Stress is a Decision

*40 Simple Ha_____ _____ Stress
and Fina_ _____er Peace*

by

Prof. Dr. Detlef Beeker

http://detlefbeeker.de/en

Prof. Dr. Detlef Beeker
Happiness Researcher

Table of Contents

Table of Contents 2

About the Author 5

Stress makes you fat, wrinkled, and dead........7

Who was the first human in history
to experience stress? 7
Why I would like to be a dog and
what this has to do with stress 9
In a Nutshell..12

The good news: We are robots 13

Why habits are better than motivation 15
Six steps to make habits 17
Four Types of habits (and why each is important) . 24
In a Nutshell.. 26

Mindfulness is a Swiss
Army Knife (#1 to #10)...............................27

Why Mindfulness is amazingly effective..................27
10 Simple Mindfulness Habits 32
In a Nutshell...55

Job (#11 to #20) 57

In a Nutshell.. 76

Relationships (#21 to #30)...........................78

In a Nutshell.. 108

Anti-stress switch: relaxed at lightning
speed (#31 to #40) 110

In a Nutshell 128

Wrap Up **129**

Free Gift...**131**

You belong to the extraordinary 3.2% **134**

**About the series
"5 Minutes Daily for a Better Life."** **136**

Disclaimer and Copyright **138**

Below is the link to my book *18 Surprising, Good-Mood Tips* (52 pages). Feel free to download it!

http://detlefbeeker.de/gift/

Do you remember the first time you fell in love? Wasn't everything suddenly wonderful? The blue sky looked so beautiful with its puffy, white clouds. You could even enjoy rain! What if you could have this lovely mood all the time?

In this book, you will learn:

- **Body parts to press** to relieve stress and improve your mood and health
- **Proven mental tactics** that will put you in a good mood in seconds
- **Secret Yoga techniques** that will easily increase your good mood
- **The unknown piece of music** is scientifically proven to be the best stress reducer
- What you can learn from **James Bond** and how it gives you relaxation and self-confidence
- How you can relax in **10 seconds**
- Practice this **mind-boggling technique** and get fresh and vitalized.
- The **best apps** to relieve your stress and give you relaxation and serenity
- The **Fidget Cube** and how it works
- Bonus: The new generation of *good mood techniques*

Download this book NOW for free so that you'll be guaranteed more joy, serenity, and happiness with the help of the best techniques.

http://detlefbeeker.de/gift/

About the Author

"The universe is friendly."

Amazon best-selling author Prof. Dr. Detlef Beeker is a happiness researcher and anti-stress expert. He has been researching these fields for more than 20 years and has written numerous books. Detlef is not just an author but also someone who practices what he writes. He has been meditating for more than 20 years.

Too many self-help guides give you big ideas but fail to show you how they are actually applicable. In his books, Detlef Beeker offers practical methods and step-by-step instructions that you can implement immediately.

At the age of 7, Dr. Beeker had already found his destiny. "I want to become a taster in a pudding factory," he told his mum. Although his vocation has changed since then, his deep desire to make the world a better place has remained.

Visit his website http://detlefbeeker.de/ to find lots of helpful tips, tricks, and a gift for you!

Stress makes you fat, wrinkled, and dead

"You can't stop the waves, but you can learn to surf."
Jon Kabat-Zinn

In this chapter...

- The first stressed man
- Why I would like to be a dog
- The best way to combat stress

Who was the first human in history to experience stress?

Strictly speaking, it was the first *documented* case. Best of all, you know the first man to experience stress. It was *Achilles*. Exactly! It was the one with the Achilles' heel. How do I know? The author *Homer* described this in his great work *Iliad*. Around 1,100 BC during the Trojan War, Achilles became the first human to come across chronic stress. The war lasted 10 years: That stress became chronic. As a reminder, Achilles was a hero and the son of King Peleus. In the movie, Achilles was portrayed by Brad Pitt. Wars are no doubt stressful, and even ancient heroes suffered from PTSD (Post-Traumatic Stress Disorder). This was evident in Achilles who felt emotionally deaf or dead. He also expressed suicidal thoughts.[1]

---

[1] Van der Kolk, Bessel, et al. Traumatic Stress: The effects of overwhelming experience on mind, body, and society. New York, NY: The Guilford Press, 2007.

Stress was harmful 3,000 years ago and remains so. There are countless investigations to prove this. This is why stress is called a silent killer. The six most common causes of death are heart disease, cancer, cirrhosis of the liver, lung diseases, accidents, and suicide. All of these diseases have a direct connection to stress. For example, stress increases the risk of heart attack by 2100%. Another shocking figure is that stress increases cancer metastasis by 3000%.[2,3] Stress makes us age

[2] How Does Stress Affect Us?" *American Psychological Association*. Accessed: August 30, 2010.

faster by weakening our immune system and promoting a plethora of diseases.

One could write hundreds of pages about the adverse effects of stress, but we don't want to be too negative. With so much lousy news, you can get in a bad mood. At this point, it is essential to know that stress is extremely harmful to our health. Therefore, we should do everything possible to avoid stress.

Why I would like to be a dog and what this has to do with stress

I would like to be a dog. My friend Felix, in wise foresight, named his Golden Retriever after the great meditation teacher Thich Nhat Hanh. Thich is always lying around. When his master is sitting at the computer, Thich isn't far from his feet under the table. I'm not sure if he sleeps or even meditates. Thich isn't worried about the future. If there is something to eat, he is happy. Whenever I visit Felix, he jumps up to me and shows me that he likes me. Even when things aren't going so well, Thich wears it with composure. He once had an ulcer on his thigh. It must have itched horribly. He got a white funnel around his neck, so he could no longer scratch. He was in a bad mood because of that? Had he quarreled with his fate? "Why is this happening to me? It itches so much! My life has been so hard! The ulcer will definitely get worse! I'm sure I'm going to die from it." I don't think Thich has such inner dialogues. He is completely stress-free and relaxed. That's why I would like to be like him.

---

3 https://theheartysoul.com/secret-weapons-against-stress/

This book is about becoming "like a dog." Don't worry. You will not learn to bark. However, the book does show you how you can reduce your stress in every situation. We fight the stress in four areas:

Mindfulness (#1 bis #10)
be here and now
relaxation
deep breathing
wide perception

Stress-off switch
(#31 bis #40)
lightning fast
stress reduction

Stress
negative thoughts
tension
shallow breathing
narrowed perception

Job | Relation-ship

Habits & tactics
against job stress
(#11 bis #20)

Habits & hacks against
relationship stress
(#21 bis #30)

- **Mindfulness:** The best cure for stress is mindfulness. Mindfulness is the opposite of stress. Negative thoughts accompany stress. We become tense, our breathing becomes shallow, and we have a cramped perception. If, on the other hand, we are mindful, our thoughts slow down, we are relaxed, and our breathing gets deeper and slower. Our perception is opened to reality. That's why mindfulness is such a great antidote against stress. That's why in this book, you'll get to know ten proven and highly effective mindfulness techniques.

- **Stress-off switch:** Sometimes it has to be fast. In acute stress situations, it is vital that we have some lightning measures that quickly relieve stress. In this book, you will find ten of these emergency aids.

- **Job Stress**: Studies have shown that the two areas that cause the most stress are our work and our relationships. This book will teach you the best techniques and tricks to deal with the two most stressful areas of your life. Thus, 85% of all employees feel stressed in their workplace. What about you? Do you feel stressed by your job? If so, the ten values and inventive techniques of this book are here to help you.
- **Relationship Stress:** Relationships can sometimes be the cause of our stress. It's second only to the stress we get from our jobs. If a relationship runs well, we can gain a lot of relaxation, well-being, and support from it. If we quarrel a lot, it is a constant stress factor. This book is mainly about partnership-related stress. However, the vast majority of tactics and tricks in this book can also be applied to other relationships.

In this book, we will address:

- 10 simple **mindfulness** habits and tricks that will help you say goodbye to stress once and for all
- 10 **foolproof** habits to de-stress your job
- 10 **ingenious** habits that allow you to let go of relationship stress and make your partnership blossom
- 10 simple **anti-stress switches** you can press to relieve stress in seconds.
- The exact **6-step guide** on how to effectively

build habits

- The secret **Qi Gong technique** that improves your mood effortlessly
- Two unknown **fun techniques** that reduce stress
- Five **smart apps** to help avoid stress on the job
- The **SOBER technique** that reduces stress at the push of a button
- The **Gibberish Trick** that reduces stress and gets you into a good mood
- The secret **ABC method to** avoid interruptions and disruptions in the job
- The simple **Mentastic trick** to get out of stress

In a Nutshell

- Stress is a silent killer. It has numerous negative effects on our physical and mental health. That's why it's important that we learn how to reduce our stress.
- Mindfulness is the opposite of stress. Therefore, it is an extremely effective tool to reduce stress healthily. In this book, we'll focus on ten proven mindfulness tactics.
- This book contains ten emergency aids to help in acute stress situations.
- Our jobs and relationships are two significant parts of our lives that can quickly lead to stress, so we will look at a total of 20 tricks, techniques, and tactics to better deal with these areas.

The good news: We are robots

"The bad habits we want, as bad people who have harmed us for a long time, to pass completely."
Epicurus

Why are we robots? Because of our life habits, 90% of the time we run on auto-pilot. Our actions are automatic and habitual. Why should this be good news? It's because we can choose our habits. We can choose those things that make us happy. Habit is effortless. If we have many good habits in our lives, then we easily have a good life. That's why it's good news. How this works is explained in this chapter.

In this chapter...

- Your habits determine your life: If you are good, your life will be better for it.
- Habits are the way to success and happiness.
- 6 steps to better our habits.
- 4 types of habits.

The goal of this book is to reduce your stress. To do this as efficiently as possible, we first look at how stress arises:

- **Stressor**: Stress begins with a stressor or a stress trigger. For example, an employee is overwhelmed with his new tasks. This may or may not be stressful. It depends on how the employee reacts.
- **Stress reactions, thoughts, and feelings**: The stressor gives rise to thoughts, such

as: "I can never do that! I'm not qualified for that!" These thoughts lead to negative feelings like fear or frustration.

- **Stress response behavior**: Our thoughts and feelings about the stressor lead to behavior. Stressful behavior is hectic, fast, and lacking in planning and overview.
- **Stress response body**: Stress manifests itself in the body through rapid heartbeat, the tension of the muscles, and the release of stress hormones.

What do we mean when we talk about stress reduction? We often cannot do anything against stressors. We usually have no control over our external environments. But we can work on our thoughts, feelings, and behaviors. There are 40 techniques in this book that will wipe out your stress. You do not have to integrate all these actions into your life. Just a few is enough. Our thoughts, feelings, and behaviors about how we handle stress have not only existed since yesterday. They have grown in the long term, and they have become habits.

The more good traits we possess, the less stressful and happier we are. That's why we should bring as many positive habits into our lives as possible.

If you want to reduce your stress level, short-term actions only help for a while. If you want to banish stress from your life in the long term, then you have to work against it in the long term.

"The most important ingredient to success is persistence."

If we want to tackle our stress successfully, we must be persistent. That sounds worse than it is, right? You just have to adjust a few screws and optimize a few of your thoughts and behaviors. That's not too hard. The goal is to change your life as effortlessly as possible. Because it should not be strenuous because that would mean more stress. Fighting stress with stress does not make sense. It is better to manage stress with relaxation and ease.

Why habits are better than motivation

Let's look at how we can achieve goals. Suppose you want to reduce stress in your life. You choose meditation as a method and intend to meditate for 15 minutes daily. So far, so good. How do you manage to meditate daily? There are three approaches to this.

- **Motivation**: The traditional method is to motivate ourselves. We realize that it is good to meditate. We build a positive feeling. "Today I really want to meditate!" The problem is often that motivation usually disappears after a few days. Motivation is a feeling, i.e., it is unreliable. Sometimes we want to meditate, sometimes not. So, if we just go for motivation, our results may not be very good.
- **Discipline and willpower**: Discipline means that we perform an act, regardless of our emotional state. That means, even if we do not feel like meditating, we do it anyway. For that, we

need willpower. For willpower, we need energy. That means it is not available to us indefinitely. On the contrary, it decreases in our daily routine. We can train willpower, but we still have some potential. Experience shows that it is difficult to sustain anything in the long run, only with the help of willpower.

- **Habits**: Habits are a great thing. Many of our daily actions are habits, and they are automatic. Brushing your teeth is an example, but also checking e-mails or constantly looking at our mobile phone. The good thing about habits is that we do not have to spend willpower. Here's an example: Suppose you want to incorporate sports into your life. Jogging for 30 minutes every day initially requires a lot of motivation and willpower. But once jogging has become a habit, you no longer need willpower. On the contrary, if you do not jog, you feel weird. Jogging has become part of your life.

  When we manage to bring many good habits into our lives, we effortlessly create a better life. However, we have to overcome a "dry spell" because habits don't become "habitual" overnight. We need to do an action regularly over a period to make it a habit. Scientists have found that action takes between 18 and 254 days to become a habit.

What is the solution? We rely on habits, but also take advantage of motivation and willpower or discipline.

Six steps to make habits

Habits are the effortless way to success. How exactly do you establish habits in your life? To do this, you use six simple steps:

1. Choose habits: Later in this book, we'll address habits that will reduce stress. Before actions become habits, we need the willpower to carry them out. Willpower is energy, i.e., it consumes itself. At the beginning of the day, we have more energy than at the end of the day. For example, if we want to bring 20 new actions into our lives, we need willpower for every single action. We cannot muster that much willpower in the long term.

So, start with **three or a maximum of four habits** that you integrate into your life. First, make a long list of the actions that you liked from this book. Be completely free. There is no problem if it's many. But then pick up the red pen and select a couple of actions that are particularly important to you. Three or a maximum of four habits are perfect for the beginning. These are the habits that you want to take effect in your life from now on.

Make sure you have selected at least one "keystone" habit. It's explained in the next chapter. It is best if your habits are well-mixed. For example, you can choose a *keystone habit*, a *mindset*, and a *micro*-habit. Or you add another *support* habit.

Tip: If you are not sure of what habits to choose, I recommend you habits #1, #2 and #3. There are two keystone habits and a mindset habit. They are very effective, and you should integrate at least one of them into your everyday life for the beginning.

2. Commit to 30 days: Take the three habits you have chosen and perform them for at least 30 days. Why 30 days? After that, these actions will have become habits in large part. As I said, actions need between 18 and 254 days to become habits. This depends primarily on how much effort they require. Doing sports for 90 minutes a day takes longer to make it a habit than to meditate in 5 minutes. The habits in this book are not very elaborate. This means that after 30 days, they will have already become 80% habits.

A few tips on how to better motivate yourself:

Stick with StickK.com: This page is about giving you an extra boost in motivation to build habits.

For example, starting tomorrow, you want to jog every day. You can deposit money at StickK.com, and you lose your money if you don't jog every day. This can be very motivating. It should be an amount that hurts if you lose it. Not $5, but rather $200. There are other ways to commit yourself. Take a look at StickK.com. It's worth it.

Motivation: Do you want to prevent stress? If you keep making yourself aware of your reasons, it becomes a source of motivation for you. There are two types of motivation; negative and positive.

- **Negative motivation**. This, by the way, is not a bad thing. It means you want to avoid something. Maybe you want to prevent getting sick, losing your job or increasing fear. This can often represent a strong drive. Think about what negative reasons you have.
- **Positive motivation**. This means you want to achieve something. For example, you want to build mindfulness and become happier or healthier.

Your task now is to take a piece of paper and write down all the reasons that come to your mind without inner censorship. You can do it in your notebook as well. It is essential that you make it free, without inner censorship. Let it flow. It does not have to be well-organized. Just write it.

Now you may have written a whole sheet or even two. Choose the five most important reasons. Of course, you can change the reasons later. Now, if you have motivational issues, you can just look for these reasons. You can hang them on your fridge, you can enter them into your mobile phone, you can display them on a regular basis, or you can recite them in the morning. You can also use it as an affirmation: This means that if you lack motivation at any moment, consider these five reasons.

3. Overcome the obstacle no. 1. What is the number 1 obstacle? To forget! The habits in this book are minor acts. They usually don't last long. It's easy to forget because they aren't part of our lives yet.

Suppose you decide to establish the habit of the "Delete Button." This is a thought-stop technique. For example, every time you have negative thoughts, apply this task. It only takes a few seconds. On the first and second days, apply it regularly. On the third day, you forget it even more often. And so it goes on until after a week at most, that you don't apply this exercise any longer. You simply forget it, which is quite reasonable. That is why we must prevent this.

Once an action has become a habit, we will not forget it. You don't forget to brush your teeth every evening, do you? What possibilities are there now to counteract the forgetting? Here are some good tips:

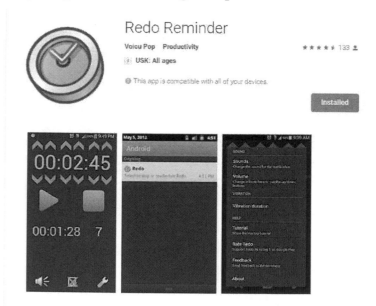

- **Reminder-App**: Some apps remind you either at certain times of the day or specific intervals. I use *ReDo Reminder* for Android. This app will certainly win no beauty prize but it is practical and easy to use.

- **Linking with existing habits**: One way is to associate the actions with other habits. You can even associate them with harmful habits. In that case, it may be appropriate to associate the techniques with stressful situations. For example, you can use the SOBER technique each time your partner grumbles at you. By the way, *SOBER* is an acronym. S stands for *stop*, O stands for *observe,* B stands for *breathing*, E stands for *expansion* and R stands for *responsiveness*. I got this mindfulness technique from Hugh Byrne's excellent book titled "The here-and-now habit."

- **Stacking Habits**: Steve Scott has proposed this technique. Stacking habits mean that we are carrying out several habits at the same time.

For example, take a look at my morning routine: I get up and do "Oil pulling." This is an old cleaning technique. Then I brush my teeth. Then I drink water with the juice of half a lemon. Then I do visualization and meditation for a short time. It is not possible for me to forget one of the steps. Once I start pulling the oil, then automatically all other actions are done as well. Stacking habits is a practical thing.

Unfortunately, we cannot apply it to all habits, since we use some habits on a case-by-case basis. It won't be of much use if we do the SOBER technique in our morning routines. It is suitable to use them now and then in our everyday life. That's why the SOBER technique for habits stacking is not suitable.

- **Visualization of the ideal day**: It is a very effective technique **to visualize your ideal day.** You can do this right after waking up when you're still in bed. Provided you are not too sleepy. If you are too sleepy, drink a large glass of water or shower first.

Visualization of the ideal day

Objective: Build motivation and remember

Technique: Imagine how to do the actions (habits) you picked out. It is best if you imagine that you practice the habits with joy.

For how long? How often? Do it daily in the morning for 2 - 3 minutes.

Tips & Tricks:

- **Visualize shortcuts.** For example, you've chosen to do the SOBER technique every time you look at your phone. Now imagine that you look at your cell phone, put it in your pocket, straighten yourself up, and carry out the technique.
- **Successful**. Imagine how you do the technique

with joy, mindfulness, and succeed.

- **No Limits**. You can also visualize other things. Perhaps you need to have a conversation with your boss, and it's already stressing you. Imagine how this conversation works optimally. You can also use scenarios such as reacting calmly and confidently when your boss criticizes you. Or you have an appointment with the dentist. You can imagine how you deal with these situations.
- **Visualize with all your senses**. Imagine the situation as closely as possible. What do you see, what do you smell, and if you can, what do you taste? The more you visualize, the stronger the effect. Do not worry about it. Sometimes it's hard to envision. Do it as well as possible, and its impact will gradually show.

4. Small steps. Don't change too much at once. Just make small changes. For example, if you want to establish meditation as a habit, start with a few minutes. Don't immediately plan on meditating for 30 minutes a day. Habits can be better introduced if there are small. It is important that you see every little progress positively. So don't say "Rats, today I only meditated for 3 minutes. Why have I done so little?" It is better to celebrate every little success. "I meditated today! I did well!"

5. Reward yourself for milestones. You can make the process of creating habits that are more interesting if you introduce milestones. An important first milestone is a *30-day commitment*. If you've kept up the new habit for 30 days, you should reward yourself. You can give yourself a big ice cream or maybe a massage. The Reward should actually motivate you. Then go on to the next milestone. The next milestone could be, for example, to keep up the new habit for another 30 days.

6. New habits. Keep introducing new habits. If you have kept up habits for 30 days, you can start making new ones. Habits are the foundations of life. Our entire everyday life consists of habits. The greater number we have of these positive habits, the better our lives are.

These six steps are proven and effective. Try them out. This allows you to easily and effortlessly establish new habits. It is important that you do it with as little stress as possible. If you try hard, try to be mindful and see where the effort comes from. All the habits in this book are effortless in themselves. If you find it exhausting, it is because of internal resistance to taking this action. Maybe you're thinking to yourself, "Oh no, not another breathing technique; I don't feel like it now." That's just too human. Introducing new actions can sometimes go hand in hand with resistance. That feels tiring, but not really. The best antidote is mindfulness. Observe your thoughts and resistances and be at ease with them.

Four Types of habits
(and why each is important)

There are different types of habits. Every habit is important in its own way. Each habit always indicates what type it is. This gives you an orientation in your choice of habits.

- **Keystone Habits.** These are particularly important actions or habits. This means they have particularly far-reaching and positive effects. For example, "Meditation." Countless studies have proven that meditation has many positive effects on the body and mind. Therefore, it's a great idea to establish this habit in your life.

- **Mindset Habit**s. This is about our attitude towards a particular situation. For example, the habit of "assume good reasons." This is a habit for relationships. Often when we argue, we think the worst of our partner. This often exacerbates the dispute. If we assume good reasons, we have more compassion and understanding. So, we have a different attitude to this situation. Getting used to this is good.

- **Support habits**. These are habits that support other habits or our goals. For example, the habit of "own interruptions." Here we use apps or other techniques so that we can work more focused. Otherwise, we are too easily distracted by Facebook or our e-mails. This habit supports stress-free work.

- **Micro-habits**. These are particularly small habits that you can easily integrate into your everyday life. For example, "the delete button." This is an effective thought-stop exercise. It only takes a few seconds, and you can use it at any time.

Why is it important to distinguish between habits? You can use the different types for the selection of habits. It is best if you have a colorful mix of types.

In a Nutshell

- The success formula is made up of small changes in the long term. In other words, habits are the way to success. Our habits determine our whole life. 90% of our actions are automatic or habitual. The question is, do we have good habits or bad habits? The more good habits, the better our lives.
- That is why it is mainly a good idea if you integrate as many positive habits in your life. This book contains 40 great habits that can free your life from stress.
- The 6-step process shows you exactly how to bring habits into your life as efficiently and effortlessly as possible.
- There are four different types of habits. They are all important in themselves. It is advisable for you to choose a good mix of the various types of habits.
- The habits of #1 through #3 are my recommendation.

Mindfulness is a Swiss Army Knife (#1 to #10)

"If a blissful mood comes over me, and I walk barefoot over fragrant grass,
wild birds sometimes forget their caution and accompany me.
When the landscape delights my heart, and I open my collar and sit quietly under falling flowers,
the white clouds gather slowly above me, without saying a word."
Huancho Darren

In this chapter

- What is mindfulness and why does it work so well against stress?
- What are other benefits of mindfulness?
- 10 ingenious mindfulness techniques

Why Mindfulness is amazingly effective

I will introduce you to what mindfulness is and why it's such a great antidote to stress. You will also learn ten great mindfulness techniques, some of which you should definitely integrate into your life. Many studies have shown that mindfulness is a potent remedy for stress. That's why I dedicate a whole chapter to this medicine. Many new forms of therapy such as *ACT (Acceptance and Commitment Therapy) or MBSR (Mindfulness-Based Stress Reduction) work with mindfulness.*

What is mindfulness?

Mindfulness means we turn our attention to the present moment. As far as possible, we are not judgmental and accept what is.

> *"Mindfulness means paying attention in a particular way: on purpose, in the present moment, and nonjudgmentally."*
> Jon Kabat-Zinn

Why does mindfulness help against stress?

That's a good question. Mindfulness is the opposite of stress, so to speak, as it is the universal remedy. Mindfulness works against:

- **Stressful Thoughts**: Negative thoughts accompany stress: "I can't do it! It is too much for me, why does my boss always dump his garbage on me?" Such thoughts often create stress. In mindfulness, we build our attention away from our thoughts towards the reality of what is. In doing so, our negative thoughts lose their strength, and our stress is also reduced.
- **Stressful feelings**: Stress leads to unpleasant feelings, such as fear, worries, and the feeling of overloading. If we are careful, we can slow down our system. We can take away the power of our negative thoughts so that our body and mind can be relaxed when the negative feelings are reduced. Also if we are careful, then we can fight negative feelings right from the beginning. If we are careless and stressed, we only notice a feel-

ing of fear when it is already strong. If we are careful, we can recognize the fear as it arises. It is much easier to fight a weak feeling than an intense one.

- **Tension**: In the case of stress, we tense our body. That's why we have cramps and headaches. Through mindfulness, we can consciously relax. This helps with stress.
- **Stressful Behaviors**: When we are stressed, we are hectic, and we do several things at the same time. It is as if time passes faster than usual. Through mindfulness, we slow down the situation. We do not eat and use our mobile phone at the same time. No, we are mindful only of one thing. We are also conscious of our behavior in general. It then becomes easier for us to notice actions that can cause stress.

Kevin was stressed at work. He was someone who found it hard to be punctual. He wanted to be at work by eight but was always a few minutes late. This doesn't matter, but he had to work very hard to arrive earlier. This caused him stress. However, he did not notice this unfavorable behavior. It was only when he dealt with his stress and mindfulness that he noticed these behaviors. He could easily have changed this by simply getting up 10 minutes earlier. Simple measures can often prevent stress.

- **Narrowed Perception**: Stress narrows our perception. We get tunnel vision. Mindfulness expands our field of perception. We perceive the whole environment and the situation. This has a relaxing and stress relieving effect.

Now let's take a look at what the advantages of mindfulness are. Mindfulness is a *Swiss Army Knife*.

What are the advantages of mindfulness?

Mindfulness has a lot of scientifically proven benefits:[4]

1. **Mindfulness is effective against rumination**: Thinking is normal. Overthinking isn't: It causes negative feelings and in worst case scenario even depression. It can be addictive. When you ponder, you constantly think about the same thing. You never come to an end or a meaningful result. Mindfulness can overcome this excessive thinking. Studies have shown that mindfulness significantly reduces brooding and depression (https://bit.ly/2HRAaJO).
2. **Mindfulness reduces stress**: The stress hormone cortisol can be decreased significantly through mindfulness. This has also been established in studies. (https://bit.ly/2HRAaJO)
3. **Mindfulness improves memory, concentration, and performance.** Here too, studies have shown that mindfulness enhances memory, concentration, and performance. Students who trained mindfulness performed bet-

---

[4] See as great book: Scott/Davenport: 10-minute mindfulness: 71 habits for living in the present moment.

ter than "normal" students. It was even noted that the prefrontal cortex, which is the front part of our brain, becomes thicker due to mindfulness. This part of the brain is responsible for the higher functions such as evaluations. (https://bit.ly/1RnltwV).

4. **Mindfulness improves our serenity**: If we practice mindfulness, we do not respond too strongly to stressors. Emotions such as anger and rage are curbed. This means we can respond to a stressful situation in a more relaxed and calm way (https://bit.ly/2GpsKj3).

5. **Mindfulness calls on cognitive flexibility**. Cognitive flexibility means we can adapt to situations more easily. So we are not stuck in our fixed-thought patterns but rather react flexibly and openly to changed circumstances (https://bit.ly/2EYlZER).

6. **Mindfulness promotes happy relationships**. A study from the University of North Carolina showed (https://bit.ly/2ovzVMo) that meditations improved relationships and assist couples to handle quarrels better. Also, the general well-being and the time spent together were perceived as more positive.

7. **Mindfulness reduces fears**. Researchers have found out something unusual. Meditation minimizes the size of the amygdala, which is the fear and stress center of the brain. This means that we aren't as scared of situations as it used to be. Our thoughts are more positive (https://bit.ly/2eigk0h).

8. **Mindfulness improves mental health**: A

study conducted by the University of Oregon (https://bit.ly/2CNwCo6), has shown that special mindfulness techniques can protect us from mental illness.

9. **Mindfulness helps with pain**. Several studies (https://bit.ly/1ULNEJS) have been able to show that mindfulness relieves pain. Pain is composed of the physical sensations plus the corresponding thoughts. These negative thoughts, the resistance to the pain, undoubtedly contribute to the suffering of the pain. If we can let go of these thoughts, pain becomes more bearable.

10. **Mindfulness improves our sleep**. Sleep disorder is a common symptom of stress. Pondering and its related restlessness prevent restful sleep. A study by David Black, among others, from 2015 (https://bit.ly/2F3moBN) shows that meditation is excellent for sleep problems and helps promote sound sleep.

Well, are you convinced? The ten best mindfulness habits below.

10 Simple Mindfulness Habits

In the following is ten very effective mindfulness techniques.

#1 SOBER

As a reminder, *SOBER* is an acronym. S stands for *stop*, O stands for *Observe,* B stands for *breathing*, E stands for *expansion* and R stands for *responsiveness*. I got these exercises from Hugh Byrne's excellent book titled

"The here-and-now habit."

The SOBER exercise is the fundamental technique. It is the mother of all mindfulness techniques. Why? Because mindfulness is about stopping, becoming aware and reacting differently.

I had the pattern or habit of being late. This has led to many stressful moments in my life. I remembered an exam a few years ago. The exam was scheduled to take place at 1 pm. I left at the last minute and did not want to be late. Students are often nervous about exams, and I did not want to strain their nerves even more. I sat in the car, and stressful thoughts emerged: "Why does this dumbass have to drive so slowly?? I'm late! That's bad!" My body tensed. I got angry because a car in front of me was looking for a parking space. I flash the headlights. The tension got bigger, I squeezed my teeth together, became angry and hectic. I was trapped in a stressed reaction. Suddenly I remembered SOBER, and I paused. I watched myself and the situation. I saw that I was tense and angry. Here the stress reaction was already interrupted. A few deep breaths made me calmer: "If I'm hectic and tense, I will not get to the university more quickly. At worst, I'll be a few minutes late. That's not optimal, but it's not that bad." I was now mindful and continued the journey reasonably calm and relaxed.

That's a prime example of how stress works. It is a habit. The most important antidote is that we stop or pause when we realize that we are in a stressful situation. If that is the case, we can behave differently. The *SOBER* technique is ideal for this. You can use it at any time and in any stressful situation. It can be used in our everyday life. This exercise is very effective and very convenient. You can practice it when driving, walking, in a dispute, even before going to bed.

Type: Keystone habit

Objective: Mindfulness, relaxation, stress relief

Action Plan

1. Stop: Pause! No matter what you are doing, stop for a moment. If you are in a car, I don't mean you should stop the car. But you can realize that you are under stress.

2. Observe without judging. What is going on in your body, your feelings and your thoughts? If you feel angry, allow yourself to feel the tightness in your chest and the heat on your face. You'll probably feel a little more relaxed when you do that. Make sure that you don't get involved in your thoughts.

3. Breathing: Breathe in and out of your abdomen a few times. Just be aware of your breath. That means you can watch how your belly lifts and lowers or how it feels to breathe in and out at your nostrils.

4. Expand your consciousness so that your whole body, the entire situation, and the context are captured. Do this in a benevolent and accepting attitude. You can also imagine watching yourself from far above. You look down from heaven on you and your situation. When we are stressed, our perception narrows. If we widen our view and give ourselves space, it has a relaxing effect.

5. Respond mindful: You have the choice on how you react. Do you let your old patterns and stories guide yourself or do you respond with care? You can be annoyed and angry with your colleague as usual. You can also get out of this pattern, perhaps when you see that your colleague is just hurt or insecure. Hopefully, you'll become more compassionate for your colleague.

When? How often? You can do this mindfulness exercise at any time.

Tips & Tricks:

- **Mini-meditation:** This exercise is a mini-meditation. The more you use it, the more relaxed you will be overall. You will see that you can deal with situations in a more relaxed and prudent manner.
- **This technique requires some practice.** You have to use it a couple of times to get it going. If you have exercise, you can apply it even in critical and stressful situations. That's why it's so helpful and valuable.
- **This exercise is fast**. You need only a few seconds.

#2 Make stress your friend

Let me introduce you to a breathtaking study. In this study from the University of Wisconsin-Madison, 30,000 people were asked: Does the belief that stress affects health play a role? The results were amazing! The scientists found that people who had a lot of stress and believed that stress was good for them had one of the lowest mortality rates. While subjects, who also had a lot of stress, but believed that stress was harmful to their health, had the highest probability of dying.

This means our belief about stress influences whether or not stress is actually harmful. Another even found that blood vessel's narrowed in people who thought stress was bad for them. In contrast, the blood vessels remained wide and open to people who believe that stress is good for them. Therefore, our belief about stress plays a crucial role in how stress affects us. Amazing!

What do we take from this? We should make stress our friend. In other words: We should have a positive attitude toward stress.

Type: Mindset habit

Objective: Positive Attitude

Action Plan

Next time you notice stress, be aware of your thoughts. Make it clear to yourself that stress is not in and of itself something negative. Stress gives us strength and energy. For example, if you have a deadline, you are suddenly focused and full of energy. At the same time stress is a signal: It shows us that something is not okay. It is a wake-up call. Stress forces us to develop new skills so that we can better deal with challenges. It is a good idea to see every situation as a challenge.

Benjamin works in a management consultancy. On a Friday evening when he was about to go home, his boss came in. "Ben, I'm sorry, we got another job. It's an emergency. Can you do it by tomorrow?" With these words, the boss loaded a stack of papers onto Ben's desk. Ben proclaimed, "Wow! This will be a challenge! Give me that!" Then a smile spread across his face, and he got to work.

Needless to say, Ben never suffered from stress. He simply declared everything to be a challenge and set to work. There is something very powerful about interpreting a supposedly negative event as a challenge or an opportunity. In NLP (Neuro Linguistic Programming) this is called Reframing.

When? How often? Every time stress occurs.

Tips & Tricks:

- **Don't forget!** It is important that in stressful situations you think of these attitudes, that stress is your friend. One possibility is to note which situations are stressful. Then consciously go into this situation with a positive attitude.
- You can also work with **affirmations**: "This situation is a challenge. I look forward to overcoming it. I will grow stronger as a result. I'll do my best at all times." You can also customize this affirmation and choose words you like better.

#3 Meditation

This is a particularly simple meditation, the Breath Meditation. Despite its simplicity, it is very effective. Meditation has many positive effects. If you want to know more about the benefits of meditation, check out this link: http://bit.do/MeditationBenefits.

Breathing Meditation

Type: Keystone habit

Objective: Relaxation

Action Plan

1. Sit in a comfortable chair or armchair. You can lean on it if you like. During meditation, it is better to sit than to lie down, as one may fall asleep easily. You can also sit on a meditation cushion or a stool.

2. Observe your breath: Close your eyes and observe your breath. Be open and curious. Be aware of how your breath enters and leaves your body.

3. Neutral Observer: Do not try to change your breath. Watch it neutrally. If it changes itself, that's not a problem.

4. Thoughts: In meditation, it often happens that the mind wanders. When you realize that you are no longer with your breath, but rather in thought, gently bring your attention back to your breath.

5. At the end: Continue to observe the flow of your breath. After 10 - 20 minutes, you can terminate your meditation. Then come back slowly into the room, stretch yourself, and open your eyes.

When? How often? The best way is to do this meditation is daily, but at least three times a week. If you have more experience, you should meditate for about 20 minutes. But if you want 30 minutes or more, go ahead.

Tips & Tricks:

- **Meditation has an incredible number of positive effects**. You are calmer, stress is relieved, fears and depression are reduced. But your body is also rejuvenated, and your immune system is strengthened.

- **I often hear: "Meditation is not for me. I am too restless."** Honestly? Everyone is initially restless in meditation. This is completely normal. And when we find it hard, we should do the meditation. It's like a couch potato saying, "Jogging is not for me. It's too exhausting." When it's exhausting, the couch potato is out of shape and should be jogging. It is the same with meditation. The more restless your mind is, the higher your motivation should be to meditate.

- **There is no good or bad meditation**. We do not evaluate meditation. We are already judging too much in everyday life. Meditation is an island of non-evaluation. If you follow the meditation instruction, then it's automatically a good meditation. Even if you have a lot on your mind, no problem. That's what happens.

#4 Practice a growth attitude

Dr. Carol Dweck is Professor of Psychology at Stanford University. She is one of the leading researchers in the field of motivation. For decades, she has been investigating the factors for success. She made a fantastic discovery. Not only talent and skills are essential to our success. An essential ingredient is our attitude. Dr. Carol Dweck empirically found out two settings:[5]

- **Growth mindset**: People with a growth mindset assume that failures are part of it. You in-

---

[5] Https://www.amazon.com/dp/0345472322/

stead see it as a challenge: "This is a good opportunity to learn from my mistakes. If I master these difficulties, I'll feel good." Failures are only seen as steps on the path to success. People with a growth mindset assume that hard work and perseverance lead to success. Talent and skills are just the starting point. In a growth setting, we assume that intelligence is not fixed. We can expand our intelligence when we learn and work.

- **Fixed mindset**: People with a static mindset assume that their ability is innate and immutable. You think things like, "I better not make any mistakes and I better look good. Otherwise, what will people think?" Failures are seen negatively and unsettling for people with a static mindset. That's why they try to avoid setbacks and to stand out in front of others.

A growth attitude leads to love of learning and resilience. It causes high activity and motivation in all areas of life, including work, relationships, and hobbies. People with a growth mindset are more successful, and resilience- and stress-free. Why? They can react flexibly to life's situation. If something goes wrong, it doesn't matter. And unfortunately, things often go wrong. That's life. If we doubt ourselves every time and go down, if it doesn't work out, we put much more pressure on ourselves than when we see setbacks as challenges. The good thing is, if you have a static mindset, you can change it. You can train your growth mindset.

"Genius is 99% Perspiration and 11% inspiration."
Thomas Edison

Thomas Edison was clearly a Growth Type. Let's take a look at what we can do:

Type: Mindset habit

Objective: Positive Attitude

Action Plan

1. Think about what type you are: You can do a test. Here is the link http://bit.ly/2jlABQu. You can also see how you dealt with setbacks and challenges in the past. Think about how you talk to yourself if you've made a mistake or suffered a setback. Do you feel insecure when facing challenges? Are you more of a security type who does not want to take the risk of failures that are too painful?

If you are already a Growth Type, then you don't have to do anything more. If you have a static mindset, it is good to change it. This will take stress out of your life, and you will be more successful.

2. Affirmation: A static mindset is a habit. It's a bunch of thoughts that come to you in certain situations. That's good news, because habits can be changed. All you need is a little stamina. This means you have to be mindful of situations that pose challenges. You can then recite an affirmation:

I am capable of doing and achieving more than I believe. I embrace challenges. I am persistent. I see the effort as the way to mastery. I learn from criticism and failures.

It is essential to apply this attitude again and again in our everyday life. This affirmation helps. Apply it several times a day for at least 30 days.

When? How often? Several times a day. Anytime you feel insecure and facing challenges. Every time you think you can't do something.

Tips & Tricks:

Would you like to know more? Then read the book by Carol Dweck. http://bit.do/CarolDweck.

#5 Three Good Things

When we are stressed, we are in our thoughts, hectic and less aware of the world around us. In the exercise *Three Good Things*, we train our focus on the positive. Every evening we write three things that have made us happy. As a result of that, we learn to see and appreciate the positive. This reduces our stress at the same time. The *Three Good Things* exercise has proven to be a very successful intervention: depression decreases, and happiness is being increased. Up to six months later, after the participants of a study used the *Three Good Things*, the positive effects were still measurable.

[6] Even in very depressed subjects who could not leave their bed sometimes, this happiness booster was amazingly effective. After just two weeks, 94% improved significantly.[7]

---

[7] Seligman / Stand / Park / Peterson (2005): "Positive Psychology Progress: Empirical Validation of Intervention", *American Psychologist*, 60 (5), 410-421.

[7] Seligman (2011): *Authentic Happiness: Using the New Positive Psychology to Realise Your Potential for Lasting Fulfilment.*

Type: Keystone habit

Objective: Training of enjoyment and mindfulness

Action Plan

The *Three Good Things* is about finding three events and writing them down. You can deepen the experience by asking "Why?" In the *Three Good Things*, there are three alternative variants, namely "pleasant experiences," "use of your strengths," and "meaningful experiences." Choose one of these variants:

1. Variant: pleasant experiences: Ask yourself: "What was pleasant today?" or ask yourself: "What was beautiful today?" Find three pleasant experiences. Of course, you can always write more, but three things are enough. You can deepen the experience by asking, "Why was that pleasant?" Here are a couple of examples.

Question: "What was beautiful today?" Answer: "I played with my little son this morning." Question: "Why?" Answer: "It was so cute to cuddle with him, as we were both happy, and it was a fun experience."

Question: "What was pleasant today?" Answer: "I rode a bicycle today. It was fun." Question: "Why?" Answer: "Actually, I wanted to watch a TV show. However, I did ride, and it was nice. I drove through a beautiful forest, which was good."

The question "why" depends on the experience. You can freely answer the *why question* completely.

2. Variant: using your strengths: This is where you reflect on three occasions today when you used your strengths. Ask yourself, "Where did I use my strengths

43

today?" You can deepen this by asking, "Why?" Here are a few examples.

"Where did I use my strengths today?" Answer: "I played with my little son this morning." "Why?" Answer: "I am a loving father and can play well with the little one."

"Where did I use my strengths today?" Answer: "I rode a bicycle today. That was fun. "Why?" Answer: "I am disciplined, and although I was tired, I still rode a bicycle."

3. Variant: meaningful experience: At the end of the day note three meaningful experiences you have had today. Ask yourself the question: "What was meaningful today?" And then: "Why?" Here are a couple of examples:

Question: "What was meaningful today?" Answer: "This morning I played with my little son." Question: "Why?" Answer: "My son makes my life meaningful."

Question: "What was meaningful today?" Answer: "Today, the sunset was so beautiful."

Question: "Why?" Answer: "It was a meaningful experience because it showed me how beautiful the world is and that there is more to it than just everyday life."

How often? How long does it last? The *Three Good Things* are carried out daily in the evening in writing. You can use it for as long as it's right for you.

Tips & Tricks:

- **What is the easiest variant?** The happiness research follows the motto "Strengthening

strengths and managing weaknesses." This
means that you should take the variant that
is easiest for you. Personally, I like the "strength
variant" of *Three Good Things*. The least I like
the "meaningfulness variant." What do you like
most? You can vary at any time. This means to-
night you're doing the "strength variant," tomorrow the "pleasant variant."

- **Writing**: It has been shown that it is best to
  make *Three Good Things* in writing. If you just
  think about it, then it happens that your mind
  easily wanders: Suddenly you're thinking about
  today's activity, where a lot has gone wrong.
  That's why the effect is stronger when you write
  it down.

#6 Affirmations

Affirmations are phrases that express what you would
like to have or how you want to be. You can apply them
to all levels and areas of life. They give your mind a
positive direction. Instead of negative self-talk, you
now have positive self-talk that builds and strengthens
you. For example, if you often have negative discus-
sions with a colleague, you can affirm: "I am completely
relaxed and self-confident in every discussion."

Affirmation is an effective and simple way to reduce
stress. They are universally applicable. I.e., you can not
only reduce stress with it, but it also gives you a better
mood, self-esteem, and improve your money management. Affirmations have a double effect. On the one
hand, they interrupt the flow of your inner negative
thought. They act like a thought-stop. Also, they give

you a positive impulse.

Type: Micro-habit

Objective: Reduce stress

Action Plan

Think about what goals you have. Do you want to improve your behavior or your thinking in a particular situation?

Alex always felt inferior in talks with his boss. He was meek and could not represent his position well. This situation stressed him. I advised him to try affirmations. He used this affirmation regularly throughout the day especially in conversation with himself. Alex said to himself: "I am cool and full of strength. I am self-confident and represent my opinion clearly and confidently!" This actually made him better able to express his opinion in conversations with his boss. His self-esteem rose, and his stress level reduced significantly.

When you set up your affirmations, you should pay attention to the following points:

1. Affirmations should be formulated in the present tense: For example, "I am calm and relaxed."

2. Affirmations should be positive. So, don't say "I am not afraid." It is better to say: "I am safe and completely relaxed."

3. Say before or after each affirmation: "... in an easy and relaxed manner, a healthy and positive way." I have this addition from the great Book "The Magical Path: Creating The Life Of Your Dreams And A World

That Works For All by Marc Allen."

For example: "I am full of vibrating energy, love, and joy, in an easy and relaxed manner, in a healthy and positive way."

How often? For how long? Work with the affirmations for about three weeks. Then see if and how they work. If necessary, you can change and adjust the affirmations.

Tips & Tricks:

- **Booster #1**: You can enhance the effect of affirmations by writing them down. Every morning, pick up a pen and a piece of paper and write down your affirmations. This is more powerful than just thinking or saying your affirmation.

- **Booster #2**: Another way to strengthen your affirmations is to put yourself in front of a **mirror**. Look into your eyes and say the affirmation. The best time for this is in the morning.

- **Booster #3**: You can support the effect of the affirmation, by placing your hand on your **heart chakra.** This chakra is located in the middle of your chest. Putting a hand on it is a calming effect.

- **You can create affirmations by yourself**. You can also search the Internet for them. A good list can be found under the following link: http://bit.do/Affirmation

- **You can work with up to 10 - 12 affirmations**. Write them on a piece of paper or use an app on your mobile phone. Say or think of your affirmations several times during the day. As a result, they are increasingly stored in your subconscious mind.

- **In stress situations, you can use the affirmation to reduce your stress**. If you have a quarrel with your partner, you can repeat in your mind: "I am calm and relaxed. I have compassion and see my partner's injury." You can even take a little break and say or think the affirmation until you're calm. For example, you can tell your partner that you want to be alone for a few minutes. Then you can retire to the bedroom.
- You can change and adjust the affirmation at any time. Feel into yourself if the affirmation fits for you in this special situation. An affirmation can sound so nice, but it's only important if it fits you.

#7 Smile in the mirror

This is a delightful habit. When you get up in the morning, stand in front of the bathroom mirror and smile big. Even if you do not feel like, if your eyes are swollen and your hairs are standing up, smile. You'll see, if you've smiled in the mirror for 10 seconds, you'll be in a better mood. This is a perfect start to the day.

Smiling and laughing makes you happy and drives stress away. Smiling in front of the mirror in the morning is a perfect way to start your day. However, this does not mean you should grumble for the rest of the day. The more you smile, the better.

48

Type: Micro-habit

Objective: Good mood and stress reduction

Action Plan

Smile in the mirror for at least 10 seconds. Do this in the morning, right after getting up.

When? How often? Once a day in the morning

Tips & Tricks:

- This habit is particularly easy to integrate into everyday life. It only takes a few seconds, and you will be in a good mood. It could not be easier.
- You do not need to limit this habit to the morning routine. You can relate them to other habits. For example, every time you look at your phone, you smile. Or in the evening after brushing your teeth, you smile in the mirror for 10 seconds. There are many other ways to bring a smile to your life.

#8 Mindful driving

My mum is almost 80 years old. She's driving an old, small, rickety car. My mum is always friendly and very warm-hearted. She is a textbook example of a granny: white hair, friendly to all, and never a bad word. I remember well when I drove her car two or three years ago. We drove behind a car that was looking for a parking space. That's why it drove slowly. We were in a bit of a hurry because we had to make an appointment. Suddenly I heard my mum shouting, "You shitface! You can't drive faster??!!"

Why am I telling this story? Driving is such a thing. As a friend of mine put it, "When driving, the evil in us comes to light." Well, that's a bit dramatic, but not wrong. I also notice it with myself. I get impatient faster when driving a car than I do normally. Do you notice that too? We curse faster. When we push, we get annoyed, and when we're in traffic jams, we get into crisis.

Studies have found that driving is downright harmful to health. It is bad for blood pressure, cholesterol levels, increases our level of stress, anxiety, blood sugar, and we develop back pain.

That's why I suggest that you drive mindfully. It helps prevent any negative effects, and driving a car can even be a pleasurable experience.

Type: Support habit

Objective: Mindfulness

Action Plan

When you get into the car, take a few deep, conscious breaths. Feel it as it enters your body, and feel if there are tensions. Try to relax this consciously.

Go ahead and become aware of your surroundings. It doesn't hurt to drive a little slower than usual. Be aware of your breath again and again. You can use stops, such as traffic light or a traffic jam, to take a few deep, relaxing breaths.

Do not play music. Set your phone to silence. Dedicate yourself completely to the driving. Be open and non-judgmental. The breath is your anchor. Return to it again and again. You'll see how relaxing it is to drive this way.

For how long? How often? You don't have to be mindful the whole car ride. Start careful driving for 15 minutes. Then you can drive mindfully longer than that. Maybe add 5 minutes every week. It is important that you feel good about it. If you stay at 15 minutes, it's ok.

Tips & Tricks:

- The essence is a mindful attitude. That means you are open and not judgmental. In other words, you are not paying attention to your thoughts.
- If, for example, when driving, the thought comes to you: "Phew, that's boring!" That's just a thought. Then return to your breathing or direct your attention to the environment. Do not let this thought take over you.

#9 Stress Checks

Sometimes we notice that a situation stresses us, sometimes we don't. Stress often creeps in unnoticed. When we are stressed, our body becomes tense, we get negative thoughts, but we do not notice. Why? Because we are not mindful. That's why it's a great and helpful habit to run stress checks regularly.

Type: Micro habit

Objective: Mindfulness, stress reduction

Action Plan

1. Stop: Stop. No matter what, stop!

2. Feel inside yourself: How are you feeling right now? Are you tense or relaxed? How does your body feel? Are you stressed?

3. Relax: Consciously relax your body. Take a few deep breaths and relax your body as you exhale.

How long? How often? Do stress checks several times a day. Whenever you think about it, do a quick stress check. It only takes a few seconds.

Tips & Tricks:

Notice is half the battle. By noticing the stress, you can release it directly. A few breaths are enough. The more often you do this, the more mindful and relaxed you become. Also note here, as is the case with all mindfulness habits, do not focus your attention on your thoughts.

#10 Sleeping Preparation

Sleep is extremely important to the body because poor sleep leads to stress and stress leads to poor sleep. If you make a habit of sleeping restfully, nothing can easily stress you.

How do you spend the last hour, before you go to sleep? Are you watching TV or checking out your Facebook page or mobile phone?

I was a bad example: I love to play chess. Years ago, I had made a habit of playing a few chess games on the internet before bedtime. Maybe you think chess is very relaxing. But not when you play bullet chess. Each player has only one minute for the whole game. You have to play fast. The clock is ticking mercilessly. After a few bullet chess games, I was completely turned on and stressed. That was the worst possible preparation for a restful sleep. Fortunately, I only did that for a few weeks.

A good, restful sleep is very essential. You can boost your sleep quality by preparing for your sleep.

Type: Keystone habit

Objective: Restful Sleep

Action Plan

There are several ways to promote your sleep. You do not necessarily have to implement all the steps that I propose below. Choose the ones that are most relaxing for you:[8]

1. Plan your sleep: Scientists have found that most adults need between seven and nine hours of sleep. However, a third of all adults do not get enough sleep regularly.

We must now calculate: Suppose you have to get up at 6:00 in the morning. It will take you about 15 minutes to fall asleep. This means you should turn off your light at 9:45 pm. Give yourself enough time and make it a habit of sleeping healthy.

2. Prepare your bedroom: It is best if your bedroom is quiet, dark, and cool. If there is still light, think about wearing a sleep mask. According to science, a bedroom temperature of 59 to 66°F (15-19°C) is opti-

---

[9] I have the following tips from the book "10-minute mindfulness: 71 habits for living in the present moment" by Scott and Davenport.

mal. If your bedroom is too loud, you can fix it with a white noise machine. What is it? Have a look at this link: White noise Machine: https://amzn.to/2vN51VE.

3. Turn off your electronics: Electro-smog does not promote your sleep. Turn off your TV, your computer, and your mobile phone. You will see that it supports your sleep.

4. Take a bath: Create a soothing and relaxing atmosphere in your bathroom. Dim the light or use candles. Use relaxing bath oils, such as lavender oil. The warm water relaxes your entire body. This is an ideal preparation for a relaxing sleep. After your bath, give your body a few minutes to cool down before you go to bed.

5. Have a light massage: Maybe you have a partner who likes to give you a light massage before you sleep. S/he could massage your head, shoulders, and back for a few minutes. However, the massage should not be too intense, but rather gentle, as this has a soothing and relaxing effect.

6. Read something light and positive It should not be a brutal mass murder thriller. Read something pleasant and positive. This fills your head with positive thoughts that you can take with you to sleep.

7. Make *Three Good Things*: See the habit in this chapter. The last thing to do before going to bed is to see what is positive. This is a great sleeping habit. You take these positive thoughts to sleep where they can continue to work.

8. Listen to soothing music: Many people have the TV running in the background. This is not a good idea, as it can make you nervous. It is better if you hear pleasant, soothing music such as classical pieces, light jazz, or relaxing music. Personally, I find *Café Del Mar* very pleasant. You can hear this music as you prepare to fall asleep. If it helps, you can even hear it falling asleep in bed. Natural sounds, such as the sound of the sea or rain sounds are also ideal for this purpose.

9. Meditation It is ideal to meditate before going to bed. Ten minutes are enough. Your body and mind can relax. Negative thoughts often prevent us from falling asleep. Meditation is a great antidote.

10. Whole-body relaxation: If you are already lying in bed, you can have a whole-body relaxation. To do this, you go through your whole body with your attention from one place on your body to the next, from your toes to your head. You start with your right foot. Breathe into it and release the tension in it. Ask inwardly if it relaxes. Feel how your foot gets heavier and more relaxed. Then go to your ankle, lower leg, and so on. Slowly relax your whole body. It may well happen that you fall asleep during this exercise.

11. Pray: Prayer is similar to meditation. It is very soothing, ideal as a pre-sleep ritual. You can give your worries and thoughts of the day to God in prayer. This way, you can fall asleep with a calm mind.

In a Nutshell

- **Mindfulness is the opposite of stress**: Our thinking becomes slower, our body relaxes, and our perception expands. If we want to escape from stress, mindfulness is a wonderful remedy.

- **Mindfulness habits #1 to #3 are particularly effective** and worthwhile. Think about it, if you do not integrate it into your life.
- **Keystone habits:** #1 SOBER, #3 Meditation, #5 Three Good Things, #10 Sleeping Preparation
- **Mindset habits**: #2 Make stress your friend, #4 Practice a growth attitude
- **Support Habits**: #8 Mindful driving
- **Micro habits**: #6 Affirmations, #7 Smile in the mirror, #9 Stress checks

Job (#11 to #20)

"The work is something unnatural.
The laziness alone is divine."
Anatole France

In this chapter...

- How to deal with your own and others' faults without stress
- How to deal with procrastination with the Solar Flaring Technique
- How to work attentively and handle difficult employees
- How to use skillful work hacks, such as "Eat the Frog," to work stress-free

A lot of stress arises from our professional life. The causes are different: We can have too much work, we can have complicated colleagues, we can have a hostile attitude to work, we are often interrupted, we have unhealthy ways of working, or we just don't like our work. In this chapter, you'll learn some very effective methods to reduce your professional stress.

#11 Use the ABC method to deal with disruptions and interruptions

Interruptions are part of everyday working life. We are called, e-mails are sent and received, colleagues come to the office, the boss calls, or customers contact us. Interruptions disturb our concentration and our focus. Constant disruptions not only affect our workflow and our efficiency, but they also make us dissatisfied and stressed. We can prevent some interruptions, and others we can't. The ABC method is an excellent tool for dealing with disturbances mindfully and without stress.

Type: Keystone habit

Objective: Mindfully handling interruptions

Action Plan

A - Attentiveness: When we are interrupted, we are mindful of it. We say to ourselves: "This is a disturbance. I will think about how I can best handle it."

B - Breathing: To prevent an automatic action, breathe deeply into the belly. Think about what options you have. Would you like to take care of the problem right now, or are you preventing the interruption?

C - Choose: Decide now in a mindful manner. How do you handle the interruption? If you reject the interruption, you can simply bring your attention back to the task. If you decide to take care of the interruption right now, that is your conscious decision. You can now calmly and attentively handle it.

How often? How long? The ABC method takes only a few seconds. You can apply it every time you are disturbed or interrupted.

Tips & Tricks:

- **You decide**: The main thing is that you do not deal with a disorder automatically and stressed, but consciously and mindfully. You determine if you will allow the interruption or not. You decide how best to handle it.
- **This method prevents stress**: Let's be hon-

est, Interruptions are annoying. Too easily we think, "Not again! I have my own things to do! That is annoying!" Such negative thoughts are not helpful. On the contrary, they reinforce our bad mood. However, if we handle it mindfully and breathe deeply into the belly, the negative thoughts will rarely arise.

- **Interruption as an opportunity**: We can see a break as an opportunity to be mindful. We take a few deep breaths and be mindful. So, we can turn a misfortune into a fortune.

#12 Own interruption

Interruptions are annoying. However, it is not only the colleagues or customers that bother us, but E-mail or Facebook can interrupt our attention. Social media such as Facebook, Pinterest, Twitter or WhatsApp can be very disturbing. If every few minutes a push-up message flutters on our screen or our cell phone "pings," our workflow can be very disturbing. Honestly? When I work, I'm happy to get a message on Facebook or WhatsApp. I immediately check to see who wrote to me and what happened. Do you feel the same way? We all tend to enjoy such interruptions. Unfortunately, it is not helpful for our flow. Fortunately, we can decide how to manage such interruptions.

Type: Support habit

Objective: Focused work

Action Plan

We need to find the easiest way is to silence our phone, close Facebook, and other websites. Unfortunately, that is not easy. That's why there are some tools that can help you.

Rescue Time: This extension for the web browser runs in the background. It tracks and documents all your activities on the computer. Later, you can see exactly how much time you spent on Facebook and how much time you spent on your work.

Stay Focused: This is an extension for your web browser. You can easily block certain websites that distract you too much. This way, you can avoid accessing this website for an hour or two.

Marinara: This is an extension for your web browser. It is a timer for the Pomodoro technique. In this technique, you concentrate on a task for 25 minutes. Then the timer signal indicates that you have a 5-minute break. Then it's back to work for 25 minutes. Follow by 5 minutes of pause, etc. This technique is simple but hugely effective. When I write my books, I use this technique. If I use the Pomodoro timer, I know that I will work and concentrate for 25 minutes. Try it, it works wonders.

These tools are beneficial. You can stay focused on what you are doing and will not be interrupted easily.

How long? How often? It would be best if you apply these tools throughout the time you are working. You can also schedule your working day. Maybe you concentrate and work for two hours without interruptions or distractions.

Tips & Tricks:

- Concentrated work without interruptions does not mean that you should also skip the breaks. Regular breaks are important.
- Concentrated work is almost like meditation. You easily get into the flow. After that, you feel good. At the same time, you are more productive and get more work done in less time.

#13 The Solar Flaring Technique

"All beginnings are difficult." Do you know this saying? There is a lot of truth in it.

Ben had decided to go jogging for 45 minutes. "Oh no," he thought to himself. "Forty-five minutes is so long. It's so exhausting. I do not feel like jogging anymore!" He did not go jogging. A few weeks later he came across the Solar Flaring Technique. It said he should go jogging for only two minutes. If he did not feel like jogging, he could stop. The next morning, Ben put on his jogging shoes: "Ok, I will manage for two minutes! Then I will see." In fact, Ben ran the whole 45 minutes.

That's the trick of the Solar Flaring Technique. We only take a small step. Imagine you have to file your income tax return. According to the Solar Flaring Technique, you just intend to work on it for five minutes. If it gets more, so much the better.

The trick works because we want to jog for 45 minutes or finally get the tax return done. With this trick we will actually jog for 45 minutes in 80% of the cases.

Procrastinating tasks generates stress. It's a burden. But we must always remember that we still have to do the task. At the same time, we have resistance or negative feelings about the task. That is why it is better to get things done right away.

Type: Support habit

Objective: Finish tasks

Action Plan

Take only a small part of the overall task. Suppose you are writing a book, and your goal is to write for two hours a day. If you can't write for two hours, then just write for three minutes. If you want to continue, then do it! If you can't it, just leave it.

How often? How long? Every time you want to establish a habit that is more elaborate, such as daily meditation or *Three Good Things*. You do that until the habit is formed. At least you should stay on the ball for 30 days.

Tips & Tricks:

The first time I heard about the Solar Flaring Technique, I was skeptical. I didn't know what was special about it. The fact is, the Solar Flaring Technique works.

These are the most important reasons:

- **No willpower necessary**: "All beginnings are difficult." There is some truth to this saying. When I'm doing time-consuming things, I find it hard to get started. If I'm supposed to write for two hours a day, that's a lot. I do not feel like starting. But if I intend to write for only three minutes, that's not a problem.
- **Likely to continue**: Once I get started, there is

a high chance that I stay tuned.

- **Puzzle study**: In a study by *Greist-Bousquet* and *Schiffman*, the participants were given puzzles. However, the scientists did not give the participants enough time to solve the puzzles completely. What do you think would happen when the scientists announced that the time was up? Did the participants stop or continue until they solved the puzzles, even though they did not have to? The result was amazing: Ninety percent of the participants stayed there and completely solved the puzzles. We humans have the urge to finish things. This plays into the hands of the Solar Flaring Technique.

- **Think in mini-units!** If you've been jogging for the first three minutes, ask yourself, "Should I jog for another three minutes?" There is a good chance that you will continue. That's better than thinking, "Should I go straight for 30 minutes?" Because then you get tense as the goal is now ten times what you started with.

- **Easily make habits:** It can be tedious to create habits. Our brain is cautious. Once habits are established, they are difficult to get rid of. The Solar Flaring Technique accustoms our brains to new, regular actions. In this way, the brain is making friends with daily jogging even if it's only three minutes. This will later make it easier for the brain to develop these habits, i.e., Jog for 10, 20 or 30 minutes.

- **Status quo bias**: This is an expression from

psychology. Man does not like change. He prefers the status quo. The bigger the change, the harder it is. The brain does not like big modifications. That's why it's so hard for us to jog every day for 30 minutes. The brain puts us in the way of resistance. It can do much better if the adjustments are small. This is not a threat. Three minutes jogging daily is not a problem for our brain. That is why small habits are brain-friendly.

- **Daily experiences of success**: When it comes to jogging for one minute a day, we can do it. Jogging for 30 minutes is something we manage to do at the beginning, but after a while, we let it go. Jogging is more and more often canceled. This is a setback and is not good for our self-esteem. Running a minute is a piece of cake. This means we have a sense of achievement every day, which benefits our self-esteem.

#14 Slow down your work

In this day and age, we often have performance pressure at work. Projects and tasks need to be done quickly. We are used to doing several things at the same time. Everything should go as fast as possible. We rush from one appointment to the next. That means stress. If we want more satisfaction in our job, we should slow down. This does not mean that we automatically give a worse performance. On the contrary, we are less stressed and therefore more efficient as faster often means worse.

Type: Keystone habit

Objective: Mindfulness, stress-free working

Action Plan

I suggest five ways on how you can slow down your work:[9]

1. Give yourself more time: Tasks should be done as quickly as possible. This is good for the company, but not necessarily for you, because it means performance pressure and stress for you. Therefore, allow yourself to spend twice as long on a task. For example, if you estimate that you need three hours for a task, give yourself six hours.

2. One after the other: We are all experts in multitasking. It is the opposite of mindfulness. This means we bring our entire attention to one thing. It also feels much better. So focus only on one thing at a time.

3. Learn to say "No": We want to be popular. That is why we say "yes" too often. To protect ourselves, we need to learn to say "no." If a colleague asks you if you can do something quickly for him, but it just doesn't work for you, you can say "No." Always ask yourself, how is it for you? You have the right to say no.

4. Excellence: Always try to give your best. It will make you feel much better about your job. Apparently, do not concentrate on doing a task as fast as possible, but as well as possible. However, please do not be a

---

[9] See Scott, S.J.; Davenport, Barrie: 10-minute mindfulness: 71 habits for living in the present moment.

perfectionist.

5. Enjoy the process: We are result-oriented. It is not so much a question of how we can achieve something, but what we have achieved. However, it is more satisfactory if we enjoy the process because we spend most of our time with the process. Let's not waste that time, but rather enjoy it. Even if the result goes wrong afterward, at least we enjoyed the process.

"The way is the goal."
Buddha

#15 Eat the frog

That is: First, complete the most difficult task. This is the frog. Why we need to eat the frogs is unclear to me. It's just an idiom.

Type: Support habit

Objective: Accomplish tasks, avoid procrastination

On a regular working day, we have a list of tasks to do. We tend to focus on the lighter issues first. However, this causes us to push the most difficult task ahead of us. It is better to tackle the most difficult task first. Then we have it behind us. That gives us energy, and we can handle the other tasks with less effort. That's why it is good to start your working day with the hardest task!

#16 Move every 20 minutes

"Sitting is the new smoking." This is a pithy saying, but it hits the bull's eye. People have never sat as much as they do today. We sit at work, in the car, and at home too. On average, we sit seven and a half hours a day. Teenagers sit even more at nine hours a day. An incredible number! Sitting is considered as dangerous as smoking! Sitting for longer periods is not good for our back. Tension and muscles are broken down. Long sitting is also a risk factor for heart, circulation, insulin metabolism, and it can even lead to diabetes. Perhaps the most shocking is that the risk of cancer is also increased. According to a study by the University of Regensburg, people who are sitting extensively are more likely to get colon cancer, uterine cancer, and lung cancer. Unfortunately, sitting cannot be compensated by sport. Even if at the end of the day, we still go to the gym or go jogging, the risk to health from sitting still remains.[11]

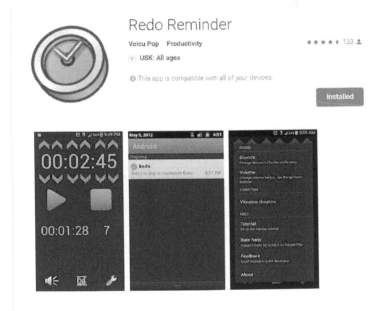

There is an easy solution: Get up every 20 minutes.

Type: Micro-habit

Objective: Stress Reduction, improve care

Action Plan

Studies have shown that you only have to get up every 20 minutes for one or two minutes. This is enough to get the health risks under control. You do not have to go around, or jog on the spot. No, just get up every 20 minutes. So do not forget, set a timer. I like to use the *Redo Reminder*. It is super simple and gets the job done.

How often? How long? Every 20 minutes for one to two minutes.

Tips & Tricks:

Take advantage of mindfulness: Simply getting up is enough. But I recommend that you take the opportunity for some stretching and mindfulness. Watch this video: https://bit.ly/NaJWt3. It takes a few minutes. However, you do not have to do all the exercises in this video. Choose a few you like. However, if you have a little more time, then it does not hurt to perform the whole exercise. As I said, it is only for a few minutes.

#17 Pomodoro

Pomodoro is awesome! A brief explanation: Pomodoro is a simple working technique. You work for 25 minutes, then take a 5 minutes break and work for another 25 minutes, and so on. That's it! But it works. After about four blocks, we should take a longer break of 15 - 20 minutes. When writing all of my books, and even now just as I am writing these lines, I work with the Pomodoro technique. I always do two blocks in a row: i.e., work for 25 minutes, pause for a five-minute pause, and then work again for 25 minutes.

Why does this technique work? For one thing, I only have to work 25 minutes. This is manageable. That's why it is easy for me to get started. Here I use the principle of Solar Flaring Technique. It takes some time, about 10 minutes, to get into a task. Only then does the flow begin. The probability of giving up is highest in the first 10 minutes. If we commit to every 25 minutes, then we stay on the ball.

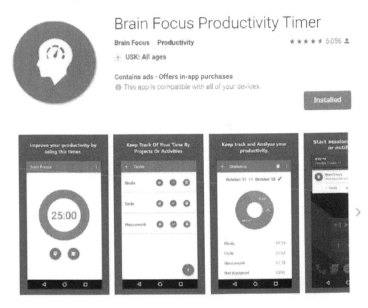

Brain Focus is a time-management application helping you getting things done! Based on technique like Pomodoro or 52/17, but you can adjust the session duration to fit your needs.

For the Pomodoro technique, we need a timer. I use the app "Brain Focus." It is simple and easy to use and does what it should.

The Pomodoro technique tremendously increases concentration. The inventor of the technique, *Francesco Cirillo,* developed it in the 1980s. Our attention span may not be that much, but we're going to get 25 minutes.

Type: Support habit

Objective: Focused tasks

Action Plan

1. Which task do you want to do?

2. Turn on the timer.

3. After 25 minutes, take a 5 minutes break according to the timer.

4. Work again for 25 minutes and so on.

5. After 4 blocks of 25 minutes, take a break of 10 to 15 minutes.

How often? How long? Every time you have a focused task to complete, you can use the Pomodoro technique.

Tips & Tricks:

What does the Pomodoro technique actually have to do with stress? Concentrated work has something meditative. At this moment, we turn off our negative thoughts and devote ourselves only to work. Then we feel good. It is also a remedy for multitasking. In those 25 minutes, we are exclusively dedicated to working. The short time is not meant for checking Facebook. That is why this technique reduces our stress.

#18 Lack of control in the job

One of the main causes of stress in the workplace is a lack of control. If our boss constantly dictates how we have to do our jobs, then it becomes stressful. If we do not have the freedom of choice but have to perform our duties as robots, then we become easily stressed.

Type: Mindset habit

Objective: Mindful and stress-free handling of lack of control

Action Plan

If you think that you have no control, and you feel angry or frustrated, try the following exercise: [10]

1. Observe your thoughts and feelings: Remember to observe them with benevolent openness and curiosity. You don't have to change them, and you don't need to go away with them either. Just watch how they come and go.

2. Observe your breath: Feel how your breath comes and goes. Feel as it moves through your body.

3. Ask yourself: What do I have control over now? Write these points down. Focus your attention on the things you can control. It's probably more than what you think. Accept the things you cannot control. If you are angry or frustrated about it, that does not change anything. You still can't manage it. You just feel worse. If you accept the situation, you'll feel better.

---

[10] This exercise is from the book "Mindfulness at Work for Dummies".

How often? How long? Every time you get angry or frustrated because you feel controlled, do this exercise. It only takes a few minutes.

Tips & Tricks:

The exercise does three things:

- On the other hand, it brings you out of your negative thoughts. You become attentive as you watch your body and your thoughts. This will make you gain distance.

- It also makes it clear to you that you can control a lot of things. Of course, you can't control parts of your work. But there are a lot of things that are under your control. You can think about your thoughts, you can move your body. You have many things under control in your private life. There are also work-related points that you can control. Maybe you can even influence things that you just assumed you could not change. Perhaps you have more leeway than you thought before.

- You also realize that you just don't get frustrated or angry about something you can't change. It is a fight against windmills. Acceptance is the wisest choice here. Life is like this: We have control over some things, and not others. Are we in control of whether we get sick or not? Do we have control over the weather, the traffic, and other circumstances ? We are not annoyed that we can't influence the weather. Therefore, we should be relaxed and get in tune with the fact

72

that we are not completely in control of our work either.

#19 Mindfulness and difficult Job relationships

Unlike in private life, we cannot choose the people we work with. There is always someone with whom we have a problematic relationship. It can be the boss, colleagues, or clients. Such complicated relationships can be very stressful. We can, however, learn to handle it mindfully. This significantly reduces our stress.

Type: Keystone habit

Objective: Stress-free job relationships

Action Plan

1. What's going on here? Find out what is really going on here. Why exactly do I find this person difficult? What are my thoughts, feelings, and physical sensations? By becoming aware of the situation, you are better equipped to deal with it.

2. Whose problem is it? We are happy to blame other people. But if we look closely, the answer may change. Do I have the problem with others, or others with me? Perhaps the "difficult" person does not mean anything negative at all. Maybe I am the difficult person. Can this be possible?

3. Practice mindfulness before the meeting: Take a few minutes to be aware of your breath and perform a short meditation. It is important that you go into the meeting openly and in an unbiased way.

Martin felt his boss is difficult: "Why does he always give me such difficult tasks? My colleagues get the easy

73

projects. But I get the complicated stuff." At the next meeting, Martin decided to be mindful. He went openly into the meeting. He raised the topic. His boss replied: "Your projects should be more difficult, because you are my best employee. I hope I can get you promoted soon." So it turns out that his boss meant well for him. Martin was the difficult person.

4. Continue to be mindful: Watch yourself and your reactions during the meeting. What thoughts and body sensations do you have? How are you after the meeting?

It often turns out that our evaluations and thoughts are the hardest part of a situation. It's not the other person. It's our negative thoughts. But if, in the worst case, the other person is truly tough, accept that. Unfortunately, you have no control over the other person. You can't magically influence their thoughts. Accept that, you'll feel better in no time.

How often? How long? Whenever you are dealing with "difficult" people, you can use this technique.

Tips & Tricks:

- It often turns out that our evaluations and thoughts are the hardest part of a situation. It's not the other person. It's our negative thoughts.
- Of course, it can also be the case that the other person is difficult. Of course, it would be nice if we could always work with uncomplicated and straightforward people. Unfortunately, this is only a wish. In reality, it is different. We have to work with difficult people. Instead of arguing

and making the situation even more difficult, we should accept this. If we make peace with this inside of us, we can deal with the situation better.

- It may also be that both people contributed to this. You are demanding, the other person is difficult, and you both are thinking: "I do everything right. Why is he so complicated?" Through Mindfulness, you'll find out what the situation is and how the situation can be better handled.

#20 Maintain maximum efficiency through mindfulness

When under pressure, we handle things differently. Mindfulness is the best choice. But we often develop resistance and stress. We are annoyed: "Why do I have so much to do again? Can't a colleague do that? This is so exhausting; I feel stressed already." Such negative thoughts make things even strenuous and harder. Wouldn't it be nice if we could work completely relaxed and calmly on a task?

It seems illogical, but in such moments, it would be better if we take a few minutes and apply the following Action Plan. It restores our inner peace, and we can find out what is good for our productivity.

Type: Micro-habit

Action Plan

1. Sit on your office chair: Turn your attention to your body sensations and breathe consciously. Close your eyes or keep them in a soft focus.

2. Observe your thoughts: Pay attention to your

thoughts without being entangled in them, as if you would watch a movie.

3. Observe your body: Pay particular attention to the areas where you are often tense. Try to release the tension.

4. Ask yourself: "What do I need at this moment to return to my maximum performance?" Perhaps it will be enough if you just relax a bit. Perhaps it is good to take a little walk or a small coffee break and have a short chat with nice colleagues. It's also possible that you'd be better working on something else.

How often? How long? Every time you feel that your performance is diminishing, do this technique. Do it regularly. It will enhance your performance.

Tips & Tricks:

- Negative feelings, tension, and overworking are never good. They damage our productivity and our health. Negative vibes consume energy. We need our energy to work. Therefore, it is better when we relax and work in peace.
- This exercise takes only a few minutes. But it can prevent hours of unfocused, tense work. It can be done while sitting in your office chair.

In a Nutshell

- Work is one of the major stressors in our lives. In this chapter, you will find exclusive job-related, anti-stress techniques. Of course, you can also use the techniques from the chapters "Mindfulness is a Swiss Army Knife" and "Anti-

76

stress Switch."

- **Keystone habits**: #11 Use the ABC method to deal with disruptions and interruptions, #14 Slow down your work.

- **Mindset accustom Item**: #18 Lack of control on the job, #19 Mindfulness and difficult job relationships.

- **Support Habit**: #12 Avoid personal interruptions, #13 The Solar Flaring Technique, #15 Eat the frog, #17 Pomodoro.

- **Micro-habit**: #16 Move every 20 minutes, #20 Maintain maximum efficiency through mindfulness.

Relationships (#21 to #30)

"Ten percent of all conflicts arise because of different opinions, and 90% because of the wrong tone."

In this chapter, we will go over ...

- How to make your partnership blossom with two games or exercises
- How you avoid disputes with the right attitude
- Fair quarrels are the nuts and bolts of a stress-free relationship

Relationships can cause a lot of stress. Together with the job, relationships are the number one stress trigger. It is not just about relationships based on partnership, but also about others. In this chapter, we focus on partnerships. However, most techniques can be applied to other relationships, such as a relationship with a colleague.

In this chapter, you will learn two techniques or habits that will make your relationship flourish, and it's all about improving your attitudes. If you can emit a positive and constructive approach to your partner, then your relationship will be as smooth as its importance.

#21 Strengthen relationships:
Update your partner map

In fact, we all know how our relationships can flourish. All we have to do is remember the beginning of our partnership, the first months, the first year of being in love. Wasn't that a good time? At that time we were very interested in our partner. We wanted to know everything about him/her.

Even if you've spent a few years with your partner, you can still do that. Care about your partner. Ask your partner how work was when he comes home. Listen to your partner sincerely. If your partner talks about her day, listen to her. Take your time. During this time, don't check your e-mail, call up your Facebook profile, or read WhatsApp messages. All of those are incredibly rude and power-based. You insult your partner when you avoid really listening to her. You should concentrate fully on your partner. Ask about the wishes and dreams of your partner. With one sentence, learn to know her. I recommend you play a partner game of "Who am I?" In doing so, you get to know your partner in a playful way closely and intensively. Knowing your partner is very important in every relationship.

Partner game: Who am I?

Type: Keystone habit

Objective: Learn to know more about your partner. This is an important basis for a harmonious relationship.

Action Plan

This game has proven itself. Play it as often as you like. The rules of the game are as follows:

1. Step: Randomly choose 20 numbers between 1 and 60 with your partner.

2. Step: One starts and asks the questions that are assigned to the numbers. Suppose the woman starts and the number 7 is the first number. Then she asks her husband, "Describe exactly what I did yesterday or the day before yesterday." If the man answers correctly, he will receive a specified score. In this case, four points. The woman judges whether the man's answer is correct. If the answer is correct, she gets a point. If the answer is wrong, none of the two will receive a score. After the man has answered all 20 questions to the best of his knowledge, and both of them have recorded their points, they change places.

3. Step: After the change, the man asks the questions. The woman answers them. The person with the highest point wins.

Questions:
1. Name two of my best friends. (2)
2. What music group, composers, or instrument do I like most? (2)
3. What was I wearing when we first met? (2)
4. Name one of my hobbies. (3)
5. Where was I born? (1)
6. What problems am I currently facing? (4)
7. Describe exactly what I did yesterday or the day before yesterday. (4)
8. When is my birthday? (1)
9. When was our wedding day? (1)
10. Which of my relatives do I like the most? (2)
11. What is my biggest dream? (5)
12. Which plant do I like most? (2)
13. What do I fear most, or what would be my greatest catastrophe? (3)
14. At what time of the day do I prefer to have sex? (3)
15. What is the best way to know me? (4)
16. What turns me on sexually? (3)
17. What is my favorite dish? (2)

18. How do I prefer to spend an evening? (2)

19. What is my favorite color? (1)

20. What personal improvements would I like to achieve in my life? (4)

21. What gift would please me the most? (2)

22. What is my best childhood experience? (2)

23. Which holiday do I find the most beautiful? (2)

24. How would I like to be calmed down? (4)

25. Who (except you) supports me the most? (3)

26. Which sport do I like the most? (2)

27. How do I prefer to spend my free time? (2)

28. How do I like to spend my weekend? (2)

29. Where do I like to order food, or which restaurant do I prefer to go to when I don't want to cook? (3)

30. What is my favorite movie? (2)

31. Which important event is ahead of me? And what do I think about it? (4)

32. How do I solve problems? (2)

33. Who was my best childhood friend? (3)

34. Name one of my favorite magazines. (2)

35. Name some of my main rivals or enemies. (3)

36. What is the ideal job for me? (4)

37. What am I most afraid of? (4)

38. Which relatives do I like the least? (3)

39. Which holiday do I like the most? (2)

40. What kind of books do I prefer to read? (3)

41. What's my favorite TV show? (2)

42. Which side of the bed do I prefer? (2)

43. What am I most sad about? (4)

44. Name one of my worries or fears. (4)

45. What medical problems do I fear most? (2)

46. What was particularly embarrassing to me? (3)

47. Which experience is my worst childhood experi-

ence? (3)

48. Name two people I admire the most. (4)

49. Which kind of clothes do I like to wear? (3)

50. Who do I like least out of all the people we both know? (3)

51. Which dessert do I like most? (2)

52. What is my office phone number? (2)

53. Name one of my favorite novels. (2)

54. Which restaurant do I prefer to go to most? (2)

55. What are the hopes, desires, longings, that I have? Name two. (4)

56. Do I have a secret ambition? What does it look like? (4)

57. What kind of food do I detest? (2)

58. Which animal do I like the most? (2)

59. What is my favorite song? (2)

60. Which sports team do I like the most? (2)

How often? How long? Play the game as often as possible. However, it should be fun. For a period of three months, play it at least once a week.

Tips & Tricks:

Stay playful: The important thing is that it should be fun. You can still develop the ambition to win. That's OK. Important: Do not see the game as a therapeutic exercise you have to do.

I hope you and your partner like the game. Try it out. You'll be amazed how much fun it is and how effective it is. After some time, you will know each other better. This is a valuable and essential basis for the happiness of your partnership.

#22 Strengthen relationships: Caring affection and admiration for each other

In a good marriage or relationship, the partners like each other. It's not always about great feelings like love and passion. No, liking and appreciating each other is the foundation. That means you find a partner charming and/or good-looking. You appreciate her voice and how she laughs. There are many possibilities. Do you still remember the beginning of the relationship? How many things did you like about your partner? After a few years in a relationship, that can be lost.

To maintain a good relationship, it is important that you like your partner and find him attractive. Therefore, learn to train affection for your partner. How do you train this? By thinking and talking about the positive qualities of your partner. You can also do the following exercise. John Gottman, the *Einstein of Love* developed it. It's a great exercise to train affection and appreciation in a simple way.

Partner exercise: What I like about you

Type: Keystone habit

Objective: You become aware of the positive qualities of your partner. By communicating it with your partner, closeness and affection are created.

Action Plan

Step 1: Sit together with your partner. Begin and find out exactly three characteristics from the following list, that you appreciate most in your partner.

What I really cherish about my partner is that he or she is so:

Active
Adaptable
Authentic
Aware
Balanced
Bold
Brave
Bright
Calm
Capable
Careful
Caring
Cheerful
Clever
Commanding
Compassionate
Confident
Conscientious
Considerate
Courageous
Creative
Curious
Daring
Dedicated
Dependable
Determined
Devoted
Diligent
Disciplined

Discriminating
Dynamic
Eager
Easygoing
Empathetic
Energetic
Ethical
Exuberant
Fair
Fascinating
Feisty
Flexible
Forgiving
Friendly
Fun
Funny
Generous
Gentle
Giving
Gutsy
Happy
Hardworking
Healthy
Honest
Honorable
Idealistic
Imaginative
Independent
Ingenious

Inquisitive
Insightful
Intelligent
Interesting
Intuitive
Inventive
Joyful
Kind
Knowledgeable
Laid-Back
Lighthearted
Likable
Lively
Lovable
Loving
Loyal
Mature
Mellow
Motivated
Natural
Neat
Nurturing
Observant
Open-minded
Optimistic
Observant
Organized
Original
Outgoing

Patient

Peaceful

Perceptive

Persevering

Persistent

Pleasant

Positive

Practical

Principled

Private

Problem-solving

Proud

Quick-witted

Quiet

Rational

Reasonable

Reflective

Reliable

Resilient

Resourceful

Respectful

Responsible

Self-confident

Self-sacrificing

Self-sufficient

Sensitive

Sharp

Sincere

Skillful

Smart

Sociable

Spiritual

Spontaneous

Stable

Steady

Strong

Studious

Successful

Supportive

Surprising

Sympathetic

Talented

Thorough

Thoughtful

Tireless

Tolerant

Trusting

Trustworthy

Truthful

Understanding

Unique

Unselfish

Upbeat

Vigilant

Warm

Wise

Witty

Worthy

Step 2: Think about why you appreciate these qualities. Think of an opportunity that catches your attention.

 Step 3: Share these three features and the event with your partner. Be calm and positive. After you've finished, your partner then takes over the next round.

How often? How long? One to three times per

week for one to three months.

Tips & Tricks:

- **Vary the properties:** Try to find two other characteristics that you like about your partner in the next round.
- **Three properties?** It sometimes happens that it's difficult to find three qualities that you value most about your partner. Be generous. Your partner does not have to fulfill this property perfectly. Be a bit flexible.
- **Only three properties?** There are couples who find more than just three properties. Just choose three at a time. You may like to take other properties in the next round.

This exercise works extremely well. Try it out. You can perform this exercise on a regular basis. This exercise is meant to help you get started. Pay attention to the positive qualities of your partner in everyday life. If you notice anything, share it with your partner. There is no objection to praising your partner. He will be happy, and will return the favor. Then you too will be praised. An upward spiral is emerging. I do not know about you, but I'm always happy every single time I'm praised.

You can make a **ritual** out of it. For example, if you're having dinner together, start eating by saying something positive about your partner. Of course, it should be sincere and come from the heart.

#23 Note the *Gottman* constant

The *Gottman Constant* has been developed by the "Einstein of Love," John Gottman. It is a constant that represents the result of a study involving several thousand pairs. Paying attention to this constant is worthwhile.

In every relationship, there are conflicts and issues. In the heat of the moment, we are not always squeamish: "You never bring down garbage bags! You are so lazy!" This is hurtful to the partner. Injuries are bad for a relationship. But we can make an injury "undone," so to speak. "We can neutralize it." We do this by considering the Gottmann Constant. It says we can undo a negative action through five positive ones. This means, if we hurt our partner once, we have to hug him five times, kiss him, say something to praise him, or apologize to him.

Type: Mindset habit

Objective: To strengthen the positive

Action Plan

The Gottman Constant refers to the ratio of positive and negative in a relationship. If the ratio is maintained at **5:1,** the relationship will not be damaged. This means an insult or criticism should be opposed to the five positive actions.

When and how often? Every time you approach your partner negatively.

Tips & Tricks:

- **Example**: Paula complains: "You are so lazy, Dennis. Can you put your stuff away? You always leave your clothes on the floor, and then I have to clean it up!" This is criticism. We humans are sensitive. We don't like being criticized. That means Paula should now say five positive things to Dennis or do five positive things, like hugging him, kissing him or something similar, so that Paula's criticism will not harm the relationship.
- So we better hold back when we criticize or are otherwise negative. It hurts immensely and takes some effort to make amends.
- It is amazing that injuries weigh much more than positive actions. But that's the way it is. Therefore, let us be careful to observe the Gottman Constant.

#24 Do you want to be right or be happy?

Fierce quarrels, in the long run, cause our relationship to go down the drain. Arguments often run like this: "It's your fault!" "No, it's your fault!" And so, it goes further into an endless loop. No one wants to back down. Everyone wants to be right. Is it really so important to be right? If our relationship has failed, do we have something that is right? No!

Being happy is more important. Don't you think so?

We all have a giant ego. We want our partner to admit she is wrong. We want our partner to say that we are right. Unfortunately, the reality looks different. Our partner probably won't say it, nor will we. As a result, the fronts harden.

That's why it's a good attitude not to want to be right in such a situation, but rather to want peace. If your goal in dispute is not willing to be right, but to settle the dispute, you will succeed. Therefore, before a dispute, make clear what you want exactly.

Type: Mindset habit

Objective: Fair quarrel

Action Plan

How can I integrate this attitude into my life?

1. Take a few minutes and think about situations in which you would like to be particularly right.

2. Choose a particularly intense and persistent conflict. Let the dispute go in your inner mind and consider whether your attitude to be right contributes to the dispute.

3. Now, think of how the conflict would have been different if your attitude were: "I want to be happy. Being right is not important to me."

4. At the next conflict, try to use the "happy attitude." This will not be easy. In our society, it is important to be right. You can use a mantra in the conflict situation:

"It's most important to me that my relationship is happy! It is more important to resolve the conflict than to be right. "

How often? How long? Every time you have a minor or major conflict with your partner.

Tips & Tricks:

- **Wanting to be right is actually unimportant**. We are right, but so what? Unfortunately, claiming right has adverse side-effects. Many conflicts escalated only because we do not want to deviate from our point of view. We want to be right, and our partner should apologize. On the other hand, if happiness is the top priority, then it's just important for us to settle the dispute and see that our partner is hurt. We open our hearts, and we can have compassion. Our partner sees that we do not insist on our point of view and can, therefore, deviate from his/her own point of view too. Once both partners have an open heart and openly hear the other, conflicts can often be easily resolved.

- **Sometimes, caution should be exercised**. However, you have to be careful here too. If only you give in, and your partner uses this to enforce his interests unilaterally, something goes wrong.

#25 Take good reasons

Anger arises when we have a need, and it is not fulfilled.

Sabine is annoyed: "You are already late: Now we have to hurry, the movie starts right away. Why do you always do that to me? Am I not important to you?" Sabine attacks Max. She is very angry. Behind her anger is the need for appreciation, security, and love. She is uncertain. Sabine quickly thinks that Max doesn't love her at all. Max, on the other hand, only sees that Sabine makes a mountain out of a molehill. He is annoyed that she attacked him for 10 minutes. "She is so bitchy and aggressive," he thinks to himself. "She does not pay any attention to my feelings at all. How can she be so rude?"

When we feel attacked, the negative motives creep in too quickly. This prevents us from being compassionate. We go into a defensive posture and counterattack. Hence a dispute can quickly arise.

There is a need behind every trouble and attack of your partner. It is often a need for appreciation, security, or love. Let's not focus too much on what your partner throws at you, but rather on the need behind it.

When Max realizes that what Sabine really wanted were appreciation and love, then he can deal with her anger with empathy and calmness.

Type: Mindset habit

Objective: Fair Fight

Action Plan

1. Think about the need for the behavior of your partner. Is it appreciation, security, or love?

2. Assume good reasons and try to be compassionate and understanding towards your partner. Do not go into a defensive posture or back out.

How often? How long? Every time you realize that you're judging your partner. Every time you're in a conflict with your partner.

Tips & Tricks:

It is not always easy to remain calm and empathetic when we are attacked. It is a challenge. If it doesn't work, it is OK. If it works, it is so much better. If you can compassionately approach your partner, the quarrel can calm down quickly.

#26 I-Messages

A little thing goes wrong, and then it becomes a big, fat fight with your partner. A molehill turns to a mountain. Why is that so? One reason is that we talk to each other destructively and hurtfully. In other words, the root of all evil is *you-messages*.

David is annoyed: "Leah, you are late again! Can't you ever be punctual? You've probably talked to your girlfriend on the phone, and you don't give a damn that I have to wait!" Lea feels unfairly treat-

ed and hurt. She counters back: "You always pre-tend like that. Two weeks ago, you were late too! But you forget that right away. We went to your friends" apartment only a bit later. Is that so bad? Your friends are more important to you than me!" The two argue, and it creates a big conflict.

What are **You-Messages**? They are frequently used in an annoying or loud or aggressive tone. They contain:

- Criticism, devaluation, or rejection
- Blame
- Punishment
- Know-it-all attitude

As a result, we feel attacked. We are offended, and we withdraw or counter. Often a dispute arises.

Examples of You-messages are: "You are always late!", "You don't give a shit!", "Everything is more important than me!"

Is it really worth it, to argue because of a few minutes of lateness? How should we best deal with such situations? The fact is, Leah was late, and David had to wait. How should David best criticize Lea? This is where a brilliant communication strategy comes into play: The **I-messages**.

Type: Keystone habit

Objective: Fair Fight

Action Plan

1. Observation without evaluation:

In this first step, it is important to talk about the pure fact to ourselves. Facts are rarely the problem, but our convictions.

Example: "We had an appointment at 8PM. You came at 8:20PM."

Important: Avoid words like "always," "often," and "all the time." They are subliminal assessments and usually make the recipient feel uncomfortable.

2. Express Feelings:

Instead of attacking the other and saying: "**You** are always late," we talk about our feelings: "I feel un-appreciated when you're late." That is why it is called "I-Messages." We state how we feel. Of course, the tone should also be fit. It would be best if we are not loud or aggressive.

Important: Many terms we use for feelings express-es an evaluation, e.g., misunderstood, abused, sup-pressed, deceived. These are not real expressions of emotion but indirect evaluations. Because of this, we should make sure that we really talk about our feelings.

3. Express your own needs:

Example: "I need security and appreciation from you."

Negative feelings arise because your needs are not

met and not because your counterpart behaves either way. So not "I'm annoyed because of your...", but: "I'm annoyed because I ... need!"

4. Formulate a request.

Example: "I would be pleased if you were on time or had told me earlier that you would come late. Maybe you can even apologize and hug me."

The request is the "bridge" through which communication with the receiver is restated.

Important: A request is not a demand or a command. I-messages are all about tolerance and understanding. Commands and demands are out of place. A request means that your partner can reject it.

When? How often? Every time a difficult or conflict-laden conversation arises.

Tips & Tricks:

- **The first two steps are so important**. Many accusations and convictions are taken out of the conversation. We stick to the facts and do not complain to others, but talk only about our feelings. This will also make it easy for our partner to understand us and open his heart.
- **Training**: If you decide to integrate "I messages" into your communication, first practice the first two steps. If you can do this

well, you can add steps three and four.

- **12 Witnesses**: We often judge others or interpret situations negatively. We say "always:" "You're always late!" or "I don't give a damn!" Is this true? Is Leah always late? Does David really not give a shit? No! These are 12 Witnesses Question: Would twelve neutral witnesses see it that way? For example, would the witnesses see that he does not give a shit? No! So, this is about objectivity and not inadmissible or untrue insinuations.
- **Would you like to know more?** This is the standard reference: <u>Nonviolent Communication</u> from Marshall Rosenberg.

#27 Practice active listening

Generally in disputes, we gladly announce our opinion. We want to explain what the other person did wrong, but we want to avoid listening to all costs. The point of view of our partner does not interest us at all. What we really need to do, both to help grow our relationship and to grow ourselves, is to listen to the other with an open heart.

Listening is not only important in disputes, but also in general. Our partner often talks to us, and we do not listen properly. We send E-Mails, or we are on Facebook. Or our partner has an important concern. Maybe we hurt our partner, and he wants to tell us. Then we may become impatient and interrupt our partner. we want to present our view of things. Listening is difficult, talking is easy. When our partner has an important concern, it is important that we listen to them.

What does this have to do with stress? Listening avoids quarrels. It's as simple as that. Quarrels trigger stress.

Type: Support habit

Objective: To ensure stress-free communication

Action Plan

The following 5 steps will help to listen actively:[1]

1. Stop your other activities: You can't listen properly if you check Facebook by the way. _Stop everything else_ and listen to your partner 100%.

2. Eye contact: This shows your partner that you are really listening. Eye contact sends a strong message to the subconscious mind. Make use of it.

3. Just listen: Do not interrupt your partner, try not to solve the problem immediately, nor give your opinion. _Just listen_. This is not always easy, especially if we have the impression that our partner makes unjustified allegations. Nevertheless, just listen.

---

[13] See Scott, S.J.: "Habit Stacking™: 127 Small changes to improve your Health, Wealth, and Happiness."

4. Wait for a natural break before asking clarifying questions: Sometimes it is not clear what your partner means. Then it is completely OK if you ask. You can also repeat the main points so that what you're talking about will be clear.

5. Be compassionate: If what your partner says is sad, try to feel it. If she is angry, share it as well. You have to listen attentively and try to understand what your partner really wants. If you cannot be compassionate, don't force yourself. But try to have an open heart.

How often? How long? Every time a partner wants to talk with you, especially if it's a sensitive issue.

Tips & Tricks:

- **Listening has positive side effects**: Through these techniques, you will become a better listener. Sometimes it is not easy, but you will also train your patience and your mindfulness.
- **Good communication is not easy**. We often talk at cross purposes. Active listening will help you understand your partner better. You'll understand why it's annoying or hurtful. Your own hard posture may also be softened. Active listening creates proximity. Sometimes it is enough to solve a problem only through active listening.

#28 Do not let conflicts escalate

Sometimes quarrels escalate. What starts as a rather unimportant problem can become a relationship-shattering dispute. This happens when the partners are not friendly and **Objective**. With really strong conflicts, it is no longer about the underlying problem. It is a matter of both being attacked and hurt. This makes it difficult to solve the underlying problem

Type: Support habit

Objective: Fair Fight

Action Plan

What can you do to prevent conflicts from escalating?

1. Take rescue attempts: Imagine that you are in the middle of the dispute with your partner. Both of you are not squeamish. But then your partner says, "Now I feel hurt." This is a rescue attempt. Your partner gets out of the dispute and the mutual attack for a moment. There are various possibilities of rescue attempts:

"Can you hug me?"

"This was mean. Can you please be more kind?"

"I love you."

"Let's calm down and try to talk more **Objective-ly**."

Maybe you hug your partner, or he might ask you, "Do you still love me?" Often we are so furious that we don't even notice such rescue attempts and simply keep on arguing. But I recommend, however, that you listen to such small signs and go for them. Or even better, be the one to send such rescue attempts. It's good to talk about it with your partner in a quiet minute. You can even arrange a code word or a special sentence, such as, "That's too much. Let's stop arguing." This is just an example. The most important thing is to be mindful. Let your partner know that you are committed to responding to such rescue efforts.

2. Take Breaks: Fierce quarrels are poisonous to a relationship. Unfortunately, we might have driven the issue to the extent that the dispute is no longer under control. Afterward, we are surprised that we have said such horrible things. In heavy quarrels, adrenaline flows through our body, causing a stress reaction. As a result, we may no longer be able to control the situation.

It is a great idea to simply take a break for about 20 minutes. Then our body has the opportunity to reduce the stress. Also, in this case, you can arrange a code word for this. "Stop! Let's take a break!" It is simple and good. Even if you have previously agreed, in the heat of the moment it is still difficult to allow a break. Anger and rage can become addictive. But be mindful that you get a break. You can take the break together or separately. See what works best for you.

How often? How long? The break should be at least 20 minutes long. This is ideal. If it is shorter, it is better than no break at all. The break should be taken if the argument becomes unattractive. The sooner, the better.

Tips & Tricks:

- **Do not let it take root!** This was the motto of my father. It says that we should try to counteract negative developments as soon as possible. For example, if we gain weight, we should not wait until we have gained 10 kg, but rather take countermeasures after one or two kilos. Sounds logical, right? This also applies to disputes. The weaker the dispute, the easier it is to stop it. The more mindful we are, the sooner we can free ourselves from our pattern of conflict. The sooner we make a rescue attempt or take a break, the better.
- **It is even better if we do not let the dispute arise in the first place.** The dispute often arises from nagging. A behavior of our partner that does not suit us. This is where the *I-messages* help. There is a high probability that a dispute will not arise in the first place.

#29 Prepare yourself before you address sensitive topics

Many conflicts arise from the way we say something. We charge each other, we accuse, we blame, we nag, we raise our voices. Our partner feels attacked, and it becomes difficult to talk about the actual problem. Now we are only arguing that we feel hurt or attacked, but it doesn't make sense. That is why it is so important that we prepare ourselves before we address a sensitive issue.

Type: Keystone habit

Objective: Avoid disputes

Action Plan

If we manage to address a difficult topic diplomatically, this is half the battle for a peaceful conversation. What's the best way to do that?

1. Identify such difficult and sensitive issues that require special caution. Maybe you are arguing more often about who's disposing of the trash. Or a partner is jealous, and it leads to constant friction.

2. Listening: If the conversation has already started, listen carefully.

3. During the discussion, you can take a break so that you can think about what to say next.

4. Take a deep breath.

5. Good Arguments: If your partner has a good argument, consider it in your answer and don't just ignore it.

6. Answer in a calm, mindful way rather than talking too fast.

7. Try to stay calm and relaxed. Resist the temptation to become emotional. Sensitive topics are often very emotional for both sides. You feel unfairly treated, your partner as well. You get angry or hurt quickly. That is completely normal and human. *Nevertheless, try to stay calm.*

If you follow these seven steps, any conflict will be soft and peaceful. Then you can talk about what the problem really is.

When? How often? Whenever a sensitive issue is to be addressed.

Tips & Tricks:

- **A dispute over trifles**: Every relationship has its difficult issues. Quite often these are trifles, and the actual conflict consists of the way we deal with each other.
- **Look behind the facade**: If our partner has an aggressive tone, he does so because he is hurt. If we fight back and also become aggressive, this usually leads to a dispute spiral. However, if we manage to stay calm and treat our partner with love, it will benefit our partner *and ourselves*.
- **Many disputes arise from past injuries**. Maybe your partner had once been

cheated on before, and that's why he's very jealous. He can't help it, but he's still suffering from this jealousy. Injuries from childhood also play a significant role. The mistakes of the father or mother are projected onto the partner. Suddenly an argument arises, and we do not know how it can be. This calls for tact and sensitivity.

- **Supplements**: You can perfectly combine this habit with "I Messages." Active listening is also a good supplement.
- **Of course, there may also have to be limit**. If your partner is too aggressive and you can no longer speak freely, it is no longer about compassion and love, but about setting limits. If you walk like on eggshells and constantly try to avoid sensitive subjects, it is not a good sign for your relationship. Compassionate and constructive communication is not a one-way street. Your partner should also be prepared to treat you lovingly and respectfully.

#30 Beware of the Four Horsemen of the Apocalypse

This term was developed by John Gottman. I referred to him earlier. He's the "Einstein of Love." Why? Because he scientifically examined thousands of couples. He can say whether the couple will stay together or not after a short conversation with a

90% probability.

The Four Horsemen of the Apocalypse are behaviors in a relationship predicting destruction. If one of these horsemen shows up, then there's a danger to the relationship. So please pay attention to these horsemen, and when they appear, try to get them under control.

Type: Mindset habit

Objective: Identify disruptive factors

Horseman #1: Criticism

If you live together, you have to complain. This is not a problem in itself, but it depends on the frequency and type. We can criticize in factually and in a friendly manner:

Lara: "I'm annoyed that you didn't wash the dishes last night. We had agreed, and it was your turn." Nagging is something else. It often gets words like "never" and "always." Lara hisses: "You never wash the dishes! You're too comfortable! You just can't be counted on!" Nagging is a personal assault and not Objective. The receiver often feels directly attacked. Either he'll retaliate, or he'll retreat. Anyway, the door is open for a bad mood and a fight.

That's why nagging is a bad idea, i.e., it's not that you should not say anything. If something goes wrong or you feel uncomfortable, you have the right to express it at any time. But please be kind and

Objective. Here, you can excellently use the "I-messages" technique.

Horseman #2: Contempt

Sarcasm, cynicism, eye rolls, hostile humor are all variants of contempt. What they all have in common is that one of them shuts down the other. He's in a superior position.

With Karl, horseman #3 liked to show up: "You had your car washed? Why don't you wash it yourself, like any sensible, hard-working person?" Then he added, "Well, you're spoiled."

This is really condescending. No one wants to be treated like that from above. It's not good for a relationship. Here too, "I-Messages" help.

Horseman #3: Defensiveness

It is only understandable that Karl's wife, Lisa, takes a defensive stance.

"I don't wash the car as often as you think. I'm not that strong, and I find it difficult to wash the car. Why are you always so mean to me? I'm doing all of the housework, and you're not doing anything."

Lisa goes into a defensive stance. A defense says indirectly that the problem is not with me, but with you. Even if the defense is understandable, it does not solve the real problem. The criticism is simply rejected without thinking about whether a true core could be present.

Horseman #4: Stonewalling

Clara nagged at her husband Sven: "You never take out of trash! What's wrong with you?" She gets louder, and her voice goes up a pitch. "You're too unreliable! My friend Beate's husband, brings down the trash every day, sometimes twice. And you? You're sitting here in your stupid chair!" Sven reads a book, seeming like his wife's tirade doesn't impress him. He doesn't look up but continues to read his book. Appearances can be deceptive. Sven cramped inwardly. But he is stonewalling. He's re-treating inside. Walls are often found in men. They feel overwhelmed and pretend they don't care. It can also be an active retreat; i.e., Sven could have left the room.

Clara feels unheard by Sven's stonewalling. Her nagging will only become more aggressive and louder. She thinks Sven doesn't care about any of it. Sven feels stressed by his wife's complaining. It would be better if he could express his feelings and talk to Clara. An "I-message" would be a good idea. "I feel pressured by you. I'm pulling myself inside. It would be nice if you could express your request in an Objectively and friendly manner."

Watch out for the Four Horsemen of Apocalypse. They're not good for your relationship. They all have something to do with unobjectionable criticism, condescension, and personal attacks. It is better to remain compassionately friendly and Objective. This will make it easier to solve critical problems. If there is a problem, such as Sven not bringing down the garbage, many couples don't want to talk about it. Clara nagged and was aggressive, Sven retired, and despite that, he still doesn't bring the garbage down. The problem is not addressed. If Clara addressed Sven in a friendly way, they could have negotiated the problem. Sven might say: "I am so tired after work. How about I get some rest for an hour and then I'll bring the garbage down, OK?" So, a problem can be solved quite easily.

If you want to watch a nice video about these Four Horsemen, see here:
https://www.youtube.com/watch?v=1o30Ps-_8is

In a Nutshell

- Relationships, whether based on partnership or otherwise, can contain major stress triggers. This chapter contains 10 effective habits. All of which are effective and stress relieving. Can I recommend a habit? Yes! I recommend #26, *I Messages*. With this one habit, you will experience amazing improvements in your relationship.
- **Keystone** habits: #21 Strengthening relationships: Update your partner map, #22 Strengthen relationships: nurture affection and admiration for each other #26 I-Messages, #29 Prepare yourself before you address sensitive topics

- **Mindset** habits: #23 Note the Gottman constant, #24 Do you want to be right or be happy? #25 Take advantage of good reasons, #30 Beware of the Four Horsemen of the Apocalypse
- **Support** Habit: #27 Practice active listening.#28 Don't let conflicts escalate

Anti-stress switch: relaxed at lightning speed (#31 to #40)

"Only quiet pond reflects the light of the stars."
Chinese proverb

In this chapter...

- 10 techniques that relieve stress immediately
- Cleansing techniques such as "Gibberish" and "Make Faces"
- Mindfulness technique "SOBER"
- Breathing techniques such as the "Vocal space exercise." The "breathing technique according to Thich Nhat Hanh" and "Alternate Nostril Breathing."
- Other well-being techniques such as "Inner Smile." "Palming." "Mentastics" and "Without head."

In this chapter, I will introduce you to ten techniques that will immediately relieve your stress. Some of these techniques are a little bit crazy, such as "making faces." These are cleansing techniques. What does it mean? You may know some forms of therapy where the clients hit cushions and shout out loud. The idea is that withheld emotions can be let out. This has a liberating and cleansing effect. The techniques "Making faces" and "Gibberish" has a similar effect. Try it out. Apart from that, there are also some proven breathing techniques. These

110

have an excellent anti-stress effect. In addition to the mindfulness technique, there is a colorful bouquet of other techniques that have proven themselves against stress.

#31 Inner Smile

This technique comes from Qi Gong. Smiling and laughter are always beneficial, even if it is not real. Even if you're stressed and you don't feel like smiling, this exercise still works. Your body remembers, and automatically after a certain period, your fake smile becomes a real smile.

What does this have to do with stress? Smile has a relaxing effect. Have you noticed that nobody smiles when he is under stress? A Smile automatically leads to relaxation and has a positive effect on stress.

Type: Support habit

Objective: Good mood and relaxation

Action Plan

1. Preparation: Relax your lower jaw and keep your mouth slightly open. Smile slightly. Even if you don't feel like, just do it like that. If you like, you can also think of something positive from your past.

2. Send smile: Close your eyes and smile to your internal organs and sensory organs. Send your smile to:

Your brain, your heart

Your kidneys, your liver

Your stomach

Your eyes, your ears

For how long? How often? Do this for a few minutes with your eyes closed. You can do it anytime when you are stressed or if you just feel like it.

Tips & Tricks:

- **Body Scan**: You can send your inner smiles one after the other to your entire body. Your feet, your lower leg, your knee. This is very relaxing and at the same time distracts you from your stressful thoughts.
- **Smile at sensitive areas**: You can also send your smile to areas of your body that are currently aching or tense. Maybe you are just having back pain, then send a warm, nice smile to your back.

#32 Making faces

The technique probably works best when you go to a very quiet and undisturbed place. This exercise serves to release tensions and aggression. In our world, and especially at work, we often just have to function. That can be stressful. Those who only work can feel cramped. We have to control each other and often enough, just grin and bear it. Can you imagine what it would be like if you did not need to be so controlled, and enjoy life to the fullest? Making faces is the homeopathic dose. It is, so to speak, freaking out gently and harmlessly.

Type: Support habit

Objective: Releasing stress, tension, and aggression

Action Plan

1. Cut out all form of grimace and facial expressions. The more extreme, the better. Just do whatever you can think of right now. You're free. Nobody is watching. Just keep it flowing. Make a good grimace. You can also tense and let go of all your facial muscles.

2. Gestures: If you like, you can intensify your grimaces with funny gestures of your arms and hands.

When? How often? Do this exercise for a few minutes. Just rely on your feelings. You'll know when it is enough. You can use this exercise anytime you feel tense, aggressive, or stressed.

Tips & Tricks:

- **Mirror**: You can also do this exercise in front of a mirror. Look how you are doing with it. Also closing your eyes is a choice.
- **You're the boss**: If you feel like jumping or dancing or moving differently, then do it. You can even make sounds, or even scream

when you feel like.

#33 Vocal space exercise

Breathing techniques work very well against stress. Why? Because our breathing under stress is shallow and fast. When we breathe deeply and slowly into our stomach, this sends a signal to our body to relax. Here's a breathing technique that is very relaxing and harmonizing. It works with breath and sound at the same time. You are intoning all the vowels. The vibrations when you sing these vowels are very soothing and relaxing.

Type: Support habit

Objective: To reduce stress through breathing, relaxation

Action Plan

1. Lie down relaxed. Put your hands on your stomach and breathe gently and deeply into and out of your stomach.

2. Vowel A: With the exhalation sing in the **vowel A**. Drag the vowel long and breathe completely.

3. Vowel E: Let the air flow in and exhale, sing the **vowel E**. Exhale completely, by pulling the stomach inward.

4. Vocal I: Let the air come in and when exhaling you then sing the **vowel I**.

5. Vowels O and U: Do the same thing with the vowel O and U.

You can repeat this as often as you like.

When? How often? This exercise takes a few minutes. You can extend up to 15 or 20 minutes. You can do them on a case-by-case basis for stress or as meditation. i.e., you practice this exercise daily for at least 10 minutes.

Tips & Tricks:

- **Falling asleep**: This exercise is great for falling asleep. Do them before falling asleep at night or when you wake up. But to be safe, first discuss it with your partner.
- **Voice Training**: If you are a teacher, lecturer, or otherwise work with your voice, this exercise promotes the sound of your voice.

#34 Gibberish

Here's another crazy technique. Why do such techniques work so well against stress? Because stress is often related to control. We tense our bodies and are controlled. To let go is relaxing. Especially when it happens playfully and freely. Here's a new language to learn. "Gibberish."

Type: Support habit

Objective: Cleaning and stress reduction

Action Plan

1. Babbling: Close your eyes. Formulate nonsensical words and sounds for a few minutes. Create your own language. Express through your babbling all the feelings and thoughts that are there right. Focus completely on your babbling.

2. Silence: Sit down and be quiet. Keep your eyes closed, and be aware of your breath or body sensations.

How often? How long? The whole exercise takes only five minutes. You can do this exercise several times a day. You can use it every time you get stressed and your head is full of thoughts.

Tips & Tricks:

- **Include Body**: If your body wants to move while babbling, let it move. You can dance, jump. Everything is allowed.
- **Up to an hour:** You can extend both the Gibberish part and the meditative part up to one hour. But in between, five minutes is enough.
- **You can't do anything wrong**: The important thing is that do not put any pressure on yourself. There are no rules. You can't go wrong. Even if no babbling is coming, this is OK.
- **Further information** can be found. at https://www.youtube.com/watch?v=cAe zOQIb4k. It is a nice and easy introduction to speaking gibberish.

#35 Palming

The exercise is simple: You put your palms on your eyes. This is an unusual exercise which is very relaxing.

Type: Support habit

Objective: Relaxation of the body and especially your eyes

Action Plan

1. Sit comfortably and rest your elbows on the back of your chair or a table.

2. Palm: Put your palms over your closed eyes as shown in the picture.

Source: http://bettereyesightnow.com/palming-requires-letting-go/

How often? How long? This exercise will take few minutes. You can use at any time you need some relaxation.

Tips & Tricks:

- **Rub your palms:** Rub your palms in advance for about one minute. This will make them warm. Then palm your eyes. The warmth has a relaxing effect.
- **On the PC**: We work a lot with computers. It's often a strain on our eyes. This is why palming is so relaxing and calming. It is important that no light reflections penetrate into our eyes at all, leaving everything to be completely black.
- **20 Minutes**: If you sit in front of computer regularly, it is advisable to relax your eyes and your body every 20 minutes. Palming is a good option here.

#36 Without head exercise

The crazy techniques are neverending. Here's an extraordinary and very effective exercise. A large part of the stress is our thoughts. They are buzzing through our heads and stressing us out. Wouldn't it be nice if we could just release all of these stressful thoughts? Wouldn't it be great if we were just free of our thoughts? Try the following exercise; you will be surprised how comfortable it is.

Type: Mindset habit

Objective: Freedom from negative thoughts and relaxation

Action Plan

This exercise is perfect for a free day. Take a walk and imagine that you have no head. When you look down at yourself, you see your feet, your legs, your stomach, your chest, but you do not see your head. You only see your head in the mirror. If you have no head, then everything is completely free. You're looking through a big oval window. How do you feel now?

For how long? How often? The best time to start this exercise is on a day off. If you have some practice with it and you like this technique, you can do it anytime. Even in a stressful meeting or a fight with your partner, you can imagine not having a head.

Tips & Tricks:

- **Do not think too much about this exercise.** It is very relaxing to imagine not having a head. There is no point in thinking about the lack of contact with reality. When you watch a fantasy movie, you just enjoy it without worrying that vampires don't exist. Let yourself fall into this exercise and imagination and pretend it is true.

- **Further information**: See this web

page: http://www.headless.org/. It goes a few steps further than this exercise.

#37 Mentastic Exercise

Stress often manifests itself through tension in our body. In our everyday life, we have to comply with deadlines, rush from one appointment to the next and are stressed out. We are goal-oriented. How about if we could let go of this stress and also our pursuit? I'll introduce you to a very simple exercise to let go. This mentoring exercise has been developed by the American physician and body therapist Milton Trager.

Type: Micro-habit

Objective: To let go and relax

Action Plan

1. Do as if you want to throw a ball: Stand upright and relax the knee joints. Imagine having a ball in your right hand that you want to throw into a basketball hoop. You prepare inwardly to aim the ball at the basket and go into casting position. The goal creates tension, and for a moment the body expresses this tension.

2. Let go: But just before you throw the ball, you're going to say, "Oh, no, not now." The right arm falls loosely. Feel the change of tension and softness. Feel how the arm slowly swings out and how liberating it feels to have no goal or purpose to pursue anymore.

3. Another side of the body: Now perform this indicated throwing motion and the sudden release on the other side as well.

4. Even freer: Ask yourself when you let go: "What could be freer, further, and even easier than this?"

How often? How long does it last? Do this exercise for each side at least five times.

Tips & Tricks:

- **Why it Works**: Stress always has something to do with tension. We want to achieve a goal, and we are tensed. This simple Mentastic exercise counteracts this. We let go, we have no goal. It is liberating.
- We feel relaxation by letting go of our body. We feel the difference between tension and relaxation. This is surprisingly soothing and pleasant.

#38 Breathing technique according to Thich Nhat Hanh

This is a particularly easy breathing technique. It goes back to the great Buddhist teacher Thich Nhat Hanh. When we are stressed, our breath becomes shallow, and we have stressful thoughts. That's why breathing techniques are generally a very effective way to combat stress.

Type: Micro-habit

Objective: Relaxation through breathing

Action Plan

1. Be aware of your breath for a few breaths. Follow it consciously and attentively.

Breathe in and say or think: "Inhaling, I know that I'm inhaling."

Breathe out and say or think: "Exhaling, I know that I'm exhaling."

Breathe in and say or think: "Inhaling soothes body and mind."

Breathe out and say or think: "Exhaling I smile to myself."

Breathe in and say or think: "Inhaling, I am aware of this moment."

Exhale and say or think: "Exhaling, I know this is a good moment."

2. Short Form: After some practice, you can also do these in short form:

(Inhale) - "In"

(Exhale) - "Out"

(Inhale) - "Calm down."

(Exhale) - "Smile"

(Inhale) - "This Moment"

(Exhale) - "Good Moment"

How long? How often? Each cycle consists of three breaths. You can repeat this cycle as many times as you want and feel good about it. Repeat this cycle three to five times. You can use this breathing several times a day.

Tips & Tricks:

- **Mindfulness**: This breathing technique works best if you observe your breath mindfully. If you have enough practice, you can just practice the short form.
- **Sleep Aid**: This breathing technique is soothing and is ideal for falling asleep.
- **Abdominal breathing**: Gentle and deep abdominal breathing is the best. Do not strain yourself. Just let it flow.
- **Other options**: You can do this breathing technique while sitting or lying down. You can also combine this breathing technique with other sentences or words. For example, you can say: "Inhale-left step, exhale-right step." You can also combine this breathing technique with activities like walking, rinsing or sweeping.

#39 Alternate Nostril Breathing

The Alternate Nostril Breathing is a Yoga technique. In Yoga, it called "Nadi Shodhana." This has a very relaxing effect. How could the yogi only invent such techniques? This technique is so unusual that usually, nobody comes up with it.

Type: Support habit

Objective: Relaxation through breathing

Action Plan

1. **Sit with your back straight** on a chair or in a crossed-legged position on the floor. You can also lie. Make sure that your head is not raised.
2. **Inhale and exhale deeply**: Inhale deeply and slowly. Exhale and let all the air in your lungs escape. Continue and relax.
3. **Close the left nostril:** Gently close your left nostril with the ring finger.

Source: http://www.sarvyoga.com/anulom-vilom-pranayama-steps-and-benefits/

4. **Inhale right**: inhale through the right nostril.
5. **Close right**: Gently close your right nostril with your thumb.

Source: http://www.sarvyoga.com/anulom-vilom-pranayama-steps-and-benefits/

6. **Exhale and Inhale left**: Exhale and inhale through the left nostril.
7. **Close Left**: Now gently close your left nostril.
8. **Exhale right:** Exhale through the right nostril.
9. **10 x**: Make at least 10 breaths like this.

How often? How long? Use this breathing any time you feel stressed or need a little more relaxation.

Tips & Tricks:

- **Works against anxiety and stress:** Alternate Nostril Breathing works well against anxiety and stress, it is very relaxing. Try it. You will immediately notice a relaxing effect.
- **Video**: Look at the alternating breathing in the following video: http://bit.do/AlternateNostril
- **Abdominal breathing**: You should breathe in and out of the abdomen all the time.
- **Fewer than 10 x**: You don't always have to take ten breaths. More or less is fine.
- This technique is very powerful. You can also use it effectively against anxiety and even panic attacks.

#40 Stop your thoughts

Thoughts are to be blamed for everything. Well, almost everything. In fact, negative thoughts are a major part of our stress. Sometimes we even start to ponder, and we think and think and think, always the same thing. Our thoughts circle, and it does not get better. This can have all sorts of negative effects, such as anxiety and depression. A simple and proven method is to stop our thoughts. When we notice negative thoughts, we inwardly say vigorously "Stop!" I'll show you an improved version. The new generation of thought stops, so to speak, and called

"Delete button."

The Delete button

Type: Micro-habit

Objective: Thoughts stop and relaxation

Action Plan

1. Imagine a button on the center of your chest or in your palm that simply turns off thinking.
2. Deeply breathe in and out three times into your stomach. Count the breaths and imagine a different color each time.
3. Now press the button and imagine that your mind becomes empty. Move with one hand, as if you were really pressing a button.
4. Pay attention to the next two breaths and bring your attention back to the present moment.

How often? How long? Do this exercise each time, when negative thoughts or feelings arise.

Tips & Tricks:

- **Baby feeling:** Try to notice the negative thoughts or feelings at the beginning of their emergence. The smaller the thoughts and feelings are, the easier we can fight them.
- **Thoughts stop turbo**: Compared to the classic thought stop exercise, this improved version is much more effective. In the classic

thought-stop exercise you simply think the word "stop." With the "Delete button" we pay attention to our breath, imagine colors and visualize a delete button. Also, we make a small movement. We actually press the "Delete button." All this is combined to make the enormous impact.

In a Nutshell

- In this chapter, you will find habits that solve stress in every situation. You can use them at any time. They last from a few seconds to a few minutes. Here are three exercises that I believe are extraordinary and may stretch your comfort zone a bit. There are #36 No head Exercise, #32 Make faces, and #34 Gibberish. Try them out. You'll be surprised how well they work.
- **Mindset Habit**: #36 No head exercise
- **Support Habit**: #31 Inner Smile, #32 Make faces, #33 Vocal space exercise, #34 Gibberish, #35 Palming, #39 Alternate Nostril breathing
- **Micro-habit**: #37 Mental Exercise, #38 Thich Nath Hahn Breathing Technique, #40 Stop your thoughts

Wrap Up

- **Your habits determine the quality of your life.** If you want to reduce the stress in your life, you should bring as many good habits into your life as possible.

- **Mindfulness** is a great remedy against stress. Mindfulness makes life better. The biggest areas of stress in your life are your work and relationships. Above all, relationships based on partnership can cause a lot of stress. But other relationships, such as professional relationships, can also lead to stress.

- Why does this book build on habits? Because to achieve goals, **habits are the best way**. Why? Because they're effortless. Only at the beginning, when a normal action becomes a habit, is it demanding. That's why it's important that we commit ourselves to doing an action daily for at least 30 days. Only then can it become a habit.

- Follow the **6 steps** to make habits. You first choose three or four habits. You practice these for at least 30 days. There are good tools for this, such as the <u>Stikk.com</u> website.

- The **number one problem** with habits is that we easily forget them. It is, therefore, important that we counteract this. You can do this, for example, through a morning visualization. You can also stack habits, and there are other good ways.

- It is good if you set milestones for yourself and reward yourself for it. The first milestone is that you will stick to a habit for 30 days. If you can do that, reward yourself. Then take the next milestone.

- Always feel in yourself whether the action has already become a habit or not. How do you recognize it? **Habits are automatic**. If an action has become a habit, it is effortless to practice it. On the contrary, when you don't practice the habit, you feel strange. You realize that something is missing. For example, brushing your teeth in the morning is a habit. When you don't brush your teeth, you feel weird. You think, "I have to brush my teeth."

- **The more positive habits you bring into your life, the better your life will be**. Start small and select three to four habits. Don't stop there. If you have made these habits, choose new habits. As I said, the more, the better!

Free Gift

"The clearest sign of wisdom is a consistently good mood."
Michel de Montaigne

As a thank you, I would like to give you a gift! Here's my book "**18 Surprising Good-Mood Tips**" (52 pages). You can download it at the following link:

http://detlefbeeker.de/gift/

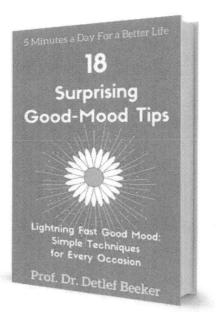

Do you remember the first time you fell in love? Wasn't everything suddenly nice? How wonderful the blue sky looked, with its white clouds. Even rain you could enjoy. What if you could have this lovely mood all the time?

In this book, you will learn:

- **Body parts to press** to relieve stress and improve your mood and health
- **Proven mental tactics** that will put you in a good mood in seconds
- **Secret Yoga techniques** that will easily increase your good mood
- **The unknown piece of music** is scientifically proven to be the best stress reducer
- What you can learn from **James Bond** and how it gives you relaxation and self-confidence
- How you can relax in **10 seconds**
- Practice this **mind-boggling technique** and get fresh and vitalized.
- The **best apps** to relieve your stress and give you relaxation and serenity
- The **Fidget Cube** and how it works
- Bonus: The new generation of *good mood techniques*
- ... and much more.

Download this book NOW for **free,** so that you'll be guaranteed more joy, serenity, and happiness with the help of the best techniques.

http://detlefbeeker.de/gift/

You belong to the extraordinary 3.2%

"Not the beginning is rewarded but only the perseverance."

Do you hear the applause? You deserve it. Why? Because only 10% of readers go beyond the first chapter of a book, and you've read the whole book! So you bring things to an end - an important skill. Also, you are among the special groups of readers who read self-help books. Only 32% do so. By the way, we have something in common. I love self-help books too! That together, you belong to selected 3.2%. Well, if that is not worth the applause!

I put a lot of passion into this book. That's why I'm glad that you found it so interesting to read. It gives me the courage to ask you for a small favor: It costs you nothing, but would help me enormously: **Would you take a minute or two of your time and write a quick review?** Two or three short sentences are enough. You can write them on the book page

http://bit.do/StressDecision

Maybe it seems unimportant, but every single review counts. Your positive review helps me continue to work as an independent author and write books that help people.

Thank you so much!

Yours sincerely

Detlef Beeker

Website of the author: http://detlefbeeker.de/en

PS: If you do not like the book, please let me know. Any kind of feedback is valuable to me. Just write me an email to detlef@detlefbeeker.de.

About the series
"5 Minutes Daily for a Better Life."

"Success is the sum of small efforts, repeated day in and day out."
R. Collier

This quote is the philosophy of this series. We don't have to do much; small actions can be enough. However, we should note the following:

- On the other hand, we must apply them in the long term. We need perseverance.
- On the other hand, we should choose the actions wisely. This is what the *Pareto principle* tells us:

Pareto principle: 20% of the effort leads to 80% of the result. This is an empirical law, which was discovered by Vilfredo Pareto. For example, 80% of a company's revenue is generated by 20% of its customers.

Isn't that great? We have to choose the means we use cleverly. So we can achieve 80% of the desired result with little effort. We can then come up with a winning formula:

Success = skillful, small actions + persistence

This formula is the basis of the series "Five Minutes Daily for a Better Life." And yes, it is possible. Change doesn't always have to be time-consuming.

Science used to think that you have to do sports for at least three hours a week to promote good health. Today we know that 30 minutes a week is enough if you train skillfully. That's not even up to five minutes a day.

Disclaimer and Copyright

and support. This book refers to contents of the third party. The author hereby, expressly declares that at the time the links were created, no illegal content was recognizable on the linked pages. The author has no influence on the linked content. The author, therefore, dissociates himself from all contents of all linked pages which were changed after the link was set up. For illegal, incorrect or incomplete contents and especially for damages resulting from the use or non-use of such information, only the provider of the page to which reference was made is liable, but not the author of this book.

Prof. Dr. Detlef Beeker

31292085R00085

Made in the USA
Middletown, DE
30 December 2018